The Politics of Essential Drugs

The Makings of a Successful Health Strategy: Lessons from Bangladesh

by

Zafrullah Chowdhury

Dag Hammarskjöld Foundation
UPPSALA

Zed Books Ltd
LONDON AND NEW JERSEY

The Politics of Essential Drugs was first published by
Zed Books Ltd, 7 Cynthia Street, London NI 9JF, UK, and
165 First Avenue, Atlantic Highlands, New Jersey 07716, USA,
in association with
the Dag Hammarskjöld Foundation, Dag Hammarskjöld Centre,
Övre Slottsgatan 2, s-753 10 Uppsala, Sweden,
in 1995.

Edited by Wendy Davies and Olle Nordberg.

Cover designed by Andrew Corbett.
Typeset in Monotype Baskerville by Philip Armstrong.
Printed and bound in the United Kingdom
by Biddles Ltd, Guildford and King's Lynn.

A catalogue record for this book is
available from the British Library.

US CIP data is available from
the Library of Congress.

ISBN 1 85649 361 X Cased
ISBN 1 85649 362 8 Limp

Cover photos: Christian Aid/Chris Steele-Perkins

This book is dedicated to:

Professor Senaka Bibile, Sri Lanka

the Hathi Committee, India

*those whose determination
led to the formulation of a
Generic Drugs Policy in the Philippines*

*those who helped formulate the
Bangladesh National Drug Policy
and continue to struggle for
better health in Bangladesh*

Contents

CONTENTS

Tables

About Dr Zafrullah Chowdhury and Gonoshasthaya Kendra

Zafrullah Chowdhury qualified as a medical doctor with distinction in surgery from Dhaka Medical College in 1964 and did post-graduate training in general and vascular surgery in England until 1971 when he left London to join the freedom struggle for Bangladesh. With his friend Dr M. A. Mobin, also a surgeon, he set up a 480-bed field hospital for the wounded during the country's liberation war against Pakistan. The following year he and some colleagues involved in the freedom struggle set up Gonoshasthaya Kendra (GK, the People's Health Centre). From the beginning, GK emphasised independent, self-reliant and people-oriented development. Its work soon expanded beyond the health sector and now includes education, nutrition, agriculture, employment generation, women's emancipation, microbiology and vaccine research and herbal medicinal plant research. Eight satellite programmes have been established in different parts of Bangladesh; together with the original centre these serve more than half a million people. In 1993, GK began an urban health programme for slum dwellers in Dhaka.

GK paramedics, the first to be trained outside China and whose experience influenced the World Health Organization's Alma Ata Declaration in 1978, are overwhelmingly women. More than 3,000 people have been trained in preventive medicine of all kinds, as well as basic curative medicine. Paramedic training at GK is recognised throughout Bangladesh as the best available and groups from all over the country send women (and men) for the two-year training programme. In addition to providing training for community-based work, the programme is now being expanded to include training for

xi

paramedics and doctors in the delivery of basic hospital services. The hospital and field programmes will soon form the base for a new medical school, designed to equip doctors, nurses and other health personnel with appropriate skills for dealing with the health problems of Bangladesh.

The programmes for paramedics and others have shown that formal education need not be a barrier to training for skilled work within and outside the health field. GK paramedics have performed thousands of tubal ligations and other operations, as reported in *The Lancet* in 1975.[1] Village women have been trained to do other work not previously seen as suitable for women in a Muslim society – for example, as machinists, welders, boiler operators and drivers.

The health programme has been able to cover 40% of the cost of preventive and curative services aimed primarily at the poor, through a combination of an insurance plan and a sliding scale of fees. The overall cost of the programme, at less than US$2 per capita per year, is extremely low and results are excellent. In the Savar project area in 1993–94, under-five child mortality was 77 and maternal mortality 2.3 per 1,000 births, compared with UNICEF estimates of 122 and 6.0 respectively in the country as a whole. In emergencies, health workers move out of the project areas to serve wherever they are needed. It has come to be expected that GK workers will be the first on the scene when disaster strikes, as in the floods, tornadoes and cyclones of 1985, 1987, 1988 and 1991.

GK is perhaps most famous for its initiative in 1981 in setting up Gonoshasthaya Pharmaceuticals under the chairmanship of Dr Chowdhury in order to manufacture low-cost essential drugs of the highest quality. Dr Chowdhury became a key advisor to the Bangladesh Government when it drew up its pioneering National Drug Policy and Drug (Control) Ordinance in 1982 which proscribed some 1,700 dangerous or useless pharmaceutical products. The example set by this legislation has, despite the pressure of foreign governments and transnational corporations, provided a remarkable example to other countries on how to control their drugs market.

The GK Trust, of which Dr Chowdhury is one of the trustees, now employs some 1,500 people full-time, with a further 1,000 part-time workers, and has a budget of Taka 440 million (US$11 million), over half of which is self-generated. Gonoshasthaya Pharmaceuticals and two other independent, tax-paying companies compete in the open market and are wholly owned by the Trust, which uses profits to support other, non-profit GK activities. GK also publishes a community health-oriented consumer monthly, *Gonoshasthaya*

(People's Health), which has approximately 200,000 subscribers all over Bangladesh and West Bengal (India).

Since 1991, Dr Chowdhury has come under intense pressure from a Government commission strongly influenced by the Western-oriented Bangladesh Medical Association and transnational interests. But the evidence indicates the drug policy has served the majority of Bangladeshis extremely well, making available at low cost a wide range of essential, high-quality preparations, although it remains true that a new National Health Policy is urgently required to complement it effectively.

In 1977, Dr Chowdhury was awarded the Independence Day Award, the highest national award of Bangladesh, for his contribution to health and family planning. In 1985, he received the Magsaysay Award of the Philippines (popularly known as the Asian Nobel Prize) for leadership in the development of community health care and the National Drug Policy. He was awarded the Right Livelihood Award (also called the Alternative Nobel Prize) in 1992.

Note

1. Chowdhury, Susanne and Chowdhury, Zafrullah, 'Tubectomy by paraprofessional surgeons in rural Bangladesh', *The Lancet*, London, 27 Septermber 1975.

Acknowledgements

I am indebted to Olle Nordberg, Executive Director of the Dag Hammarskjöld Foundation, whose patience, persistence and encouragement helped me to write this book. I am also grateful to the Dag Hammarskjöld Foundation for its support for my work.

The late Sister Judy Saul, from the USA, who was a volunteer radiographer at Gonoshasthaya Kendra, worked continuously for 14 nights in 1982 to type up all the documents of the National Drug Policy (NDP) of Bangladesh. She also helped promote issues related to the NDP among church groups in the USA. During 1982–86, Dr Susanne Ehrhardt Chowdhury encouraged me continuously to withstand pressure from various vested-interest groups trying to dismantle the NDP. She inspired me intellectually and preserved many documents related to the NDP. Without the help of Sister Judy Saul and Dr Susanne Chowdhury in maintaining the confidentiality of the NDP documents during their preparation phase, their publication at the time would not have been possible.

Steve Minkin, formerly of Unicef, Bangladesh, and now living in the USA, helped me to procure declassified documents from the US government. He worked hard to persuade US scientists and consumer bodies to actively support the Bangladesh National Drug Policy.

Dr Quasem Chowdhury, Executive Director of Gonoshasthaya Kendra, and the other staff members of GK took on the extra burden of my regular duties to free me to write this book. My mother-in-law, Zaheda Khanum, not only provided me with hospitality and a quiet space in Dhaka in which to write the book but also endured my temperament with affection.

Shireen Huq, a pioneer of the women's movement in Bangladesh, and a loving wife, gave me constant encouragement and regularly monitored the book's progress. Without her, this book would not have become a reality.

ACKNOWLEDGEMENTS

Special thanks to Sk. Sajedur Rahman of Health for All, who provided me with newspaper clippings and much useful information. I also appreciate the hard work of Abdullah Al Shafi who transferred the written text on to computer.

The most valuable assistance of Andrew Chetley in the editing of the final chapter of the book is warmly acknowledged, as is his patient and good-humoured support throughout the editing process. In contributing in various ways to the final stages of preparation for publication, the assistance and hard work of Gerd Ericson, Kerstin Kvist and Jason Pearce are likewise gratefully acknowledged.

The final word is always the editor's. Finally, I express my most grateful thanks to my editor, Wendy Davies, who carefully and critically went through the manuscript several times.

Zafrullah Chowdhury

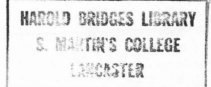

Preface
Susan George

Achieving anything simple is always complicated. It's usually exhausting, sometimes heroic as well. *The Politics of Essential Drugs* provides an excellent case in point. At first blush, one might assume that the provision of safe, effective, low-cost medicines to the population would rank high among any nation's health priorities and enjoy the favour of the authorities of Bangladesh or anywhere else. One would be wrong.

It's not enough that the most effective essential drugs have been repeatedly identified nor that the technology to produce them efficiently and cheaply exists; it doesn't even matter that the financial savings to the nation would be huge and countless lives could be saved. The country as a whole would benefit immensely, yes, but – here the tale becomes drearily familiar – when transnational corporations (TNCs) and cosseted professional interests risk the merest loss, then prepare for the energy-draining, nerve-fraying, patience-of-a-saint-trying long haul.

While Zafrullah Chowdhury's patience has surely been tried, he would just as surely resist anyone's attempting to thrust a halo upon him. Perhaps he will, however, let it be said that he has maintained his energy and kept his nerve in the face of obstacles as devious in their underhandedness as they have been baroque in their complexity. This book chronicles a long, as-yet-unfinished struggle to design a rational drug policy for his country.

The first part of *The Politics of Essential Drugs* is just the sort of summary needed by non-specialists in order to bring them up to speed. If, like me, you knew that the world-wide health and pharmaceuticals situation is bad but you weren't sure how bad, you will be enlightened, if that's the word. The drug scene (the *legal* drug scene, that is) is nothing short of scandalous, even in the presumably law-abiding, antiseptic and carefully regulated societies of the North. Though the message of this chapter is not, perhaps, a Dantesque placard bidding us Abandon Hope, we should still recognise the exorbitant privileges already forfeited to the TNCs and the difficulties of clawing them back.

In the so-called Third World – this vast realm of the under-regulated and the over-exploited – the sway of the drug companies is virtually beyond belief. As becomes abundantly clear in these pages, they will do whatever it takes to make sure it remains so. No country is too poor, no market too insignificant: the pharmaceuticals giants defend their interests on every front, against all comers.

Part of Chowdhury's description of these manoeuvres may strike some readers as over-detailed: it did me, at first, but then I recognised that I should beware of this initial reaction. His careful rendering of the intricate machinations of the interests aligned against any reasonable outcome of a National Drug Policy is a primer for the forgetful: only transpose, and you will see in his text the names of your own local potentates, in full cry against the humane or the rational.

Do not presume, then, that because you are not a Bangladeshi, you have no need to know what this Minister or national commission did when; how the press reacted, informed or pressured by interest x or y, under such or such conditions and circumstances. Chowdhury's narrative stands for every country; the pages you may be tempted to skip concern every patriot who intends to try, now or in the future, to buck the system and to put the people's interests before those of the venal and the powerful.

The devil, they say, is in the details, and so is international capitalism. We can only understand the mechanics of its relentless drive for profits when given, as we are given here, chapter and verse of its incredible will to prevent a useful, benevolent allocation of a poor country's meagre resources.

Chowdhury doesn't leave anyone out; no-one escapes from these pages unscathed: neither the American Ambassador as leader of the storm-troopers defending the turf of the TNCs, nor the traditional rip-off artists practising spurious and lucrative versions of 'Ayurvedic' medicine on the backs of poor and illiterate people. Doctors are not spared, though some may be simply innocent victims themselves. They get no training whatsoever in the economics of the drug trade, and are constantly plied by the companies with a plethora of juicy inducements in many forms: free travel, stipends, gifts, opportunities for publication, for which the encompassing word is *bribes*.

Most members of the medical profession are willing middle-men and women for drug companies whose attitude can be summarised as 'what they don't know won't hurt them' – although it may be devastating for their patients. The World Health Organization – which should be the international refuge of the virtuous – has not always helped, and has sometimes harmed. *Et tu*, WHO, which must also look to its bottom line and avoid offence to its top contributors, the United States first among them.

Let me now, at the end, declare an interest. It happens that, at the invitation of Zafrullah Chowdhury, I made my first and only visit to Bangladesh to participate in a conference on 'Transfer of Technology' at his Savar Centre and visit the resplendent new Gonoshasthaya Kendra (GK) pharmaceuticals factory at its official consecration in January 1982. I had the opportunity to witness some of the aspects of an alternative health policy at first hand, following, for example, one itinerant Savar health worker in her daily rounds, including a tubal ligature performed under perfectly hygienic conditions in a simple village clinic on a woman who had borne all the children she wanted.

I also witnessed, from a distance, a pitched battle between the hired thugs of local landowners – on whom it had suddenly dawned that the land they had ceded to GK was actually worth something – and the staff of the Savar Centre. I wasn't there, but I wasn't surprised either when the arson attempt was made on the pharmaceuticals plant. I'm afraid Chowdhury describes the courage and heroism of the staff (not to mention his own), many of whom were wounded defending the factory, far too briefly and modestly here. This may be because physical and political violence is the daily bread of the health professionals trying to institute another kind of care; just as it is the lot of those trying to inscribe an alternative drug policy in the national statute books.

Depressing reading, this book? Yes and no. Sisyphus's boulder must ever be pushed up the mountain, but still, it seems slowly to be wearing a groove to the summit. Chowdhury knows as much as anyone about this unending upward push. His book told me once more what I know to be true, but of which, like most of us, I must be constantly reminded. Decent people (and I count myself self-indulgently among them) sometimes simply cannot grasp the lengths to which corporations and those who support them are prepared to go in the pursuit of power and profit. Study this exceptionally fertile case. It will stand you in good stead when you struggle for simple justice in the field of health or any other, wherever you may live.

1

The global drug situation

Bangladesh has been one of the pioneers in formulating and implementing a National Drug Policy in the face of the massively powerful and lucrative global pharmaceutical industry. Like other countries which have sought to improve the health of their citizens by controlling the provision and use of drugs, it has had to stand up resolutely to the transnational companies (TNCs), which are concerned less with promoting health and curing disease than with amassing huge profits. Moreover, the governments and politicians of industrialised countries have almost invariably taken sides with their TNCs against attempts in the Third World and elsewhere to rationalise pharmaceutical operations. Opposition to reform has also come from national medical associations, often working in collusion with TNCs: in Australia, New Zealand and the USA, as in India, Sri Lanka and Bangladesh, vested interests within the medical profession play a powerful role in countering efforts to introduce and consolidate rational and cost-effective pharmaceutical policies.

A brief survey reveals the extent to which the most powerful TNCs control the global drug market. In 1992–93, the top five TNCs accounted for almost one-fifth (18 per cent) of total pharmaceutical sales; the top ten companies enjoyed 31 per cent and the top 20 more than 50 per cent of global sales. Profits over sales varied from 25 per cent to just over 37 per cent, with Merck at 37.1 per cent, Glaxo at 34 per cent and the US generic company Mylan at 33.3 per cent.[1] The top companies' sales in foreign countries varied from 55.8 to 89.7 per cent, while 95 per cent of the sales of the Swiss companies Ciba-Geigy, Roche and Sandoz were to overseas markets.[2]

The pharmaceutical industry is as corrupt as it is powerful. As Australian criminologist Professor John Braithwaite has shown, it has a worse record of bribery and corruption than any other industry and a disturbing history of criminal negligence in the manufacture of drugs and of fraudulent practice in the area of safety-testing.[3]

Expenditure on drugs

Global expenditure on pharmaceuticals is estimated to be US$220 billion per annum, yet two billion people in the world have no regular access to drugs.[4] Industrialised countries, with 25 per cent of the world's population, consume 86 per cent of the world's total drug supply, while the 75 per cent of the world's population living in Third World countries consume the remaining 14 per cent. Per capita expenditure on drugs varies widely from country to country, ranging from US$2 in Bangladesh to US$400 in Japan (Table 1.1). Most Third World countries spend between 22 per cent and over 60 per cent of their total health budget on drugs,[5] while the proportion is between 8 and 10 per cent in the case of all industrialised countries except Japan.

Table 1.1:   Annual drug expenditure per capita in 1990 in selected countries

Country	Per capita expenditure (US$)
Japan	400
Germany	215
Canada	121
United Kingdom	95
Chile	29
Mexico	27
Turkey	21
Morocco	17
Brazil	16
Philippines	11
Ghana	9
China	7
Pakistan	7
Indonesia	5
Kenya	4
India	3
Mozambique	2
Bangladesh	2

Source: Pallance R., Pagany J. and Forstner H., *The World's Pharmaceutical Industries: An International Perspective on Innovation, Competition and Policy,* Edward Elgar Publishing Ltd, 1992.

Unnecessary, ineffective and harmful drugs

The number of brands per drug varies greatly from one country to another. Third World countries, with the least developed regulatory apparatus and quality control mechanisms, have the highest number of brands. In 1994, Norway had only about 2,600, the UK about 6,500, and Germany, Italy and Spain around 10,000, while Brazil had 20,000, and India over 50,000.

Irrational drug use is directly related to the number of brands on the market and to their promotion. At various points over the last three and a half decades, a number of countries in both the North and the South have set up committees and commissions to investigate the pharmaceuticals market: without exception their findings have been extremely disturbing.

Contrary to the popular belief that large profits are required to finance long-term research into new and useful drugs, almost the reverse situation prevails. As far back as 1959, the Public Accounts Committee of the UK described the excessive profits of the drug companies as an inducement to produce unnecessary variations of existing preparations.[6] In 1965, the Sainsbury Committee appointed by the UK Government found 35 per cent of the 2,241 drugs then available on the market to be 'obsolete, ineffective or irrational combinations'.[7] Nearly two decades later, in 1983, the British Joint Formulary Committee (comprised of members of the British Medical Association and the Pharmaceutical Society of Great Britain) found that 22–24 per cent of available drugs were of 'uncertain', 'doubtful' or 'little' value.[8]

The first investigation into the pharmaceuticals market in a Third World country was carried out by the Hathi Committee, formed in February 1974 by the Government of India and chaired by Jaisukhlal Hathi. One of its principal conclusions was that brand names were responsible for the large number of unnecessary and often irrational formulations on the market.[9]

Exaggerated and misleading claims

Determined promotion by the drug companies, more often than not involving exaggerated and misleading claims for the therapeutic qualities of their products, has led to overprescribing and misprescribing of medicines by doctors in both industrialised and Third World countries. At the instigation of President Lyndon Johnson, the US Department of Health, Education and Welfare established the Task Force on Prescription Drugs in 1967 to investigate the alarming situtation.[10]

The task force carried out two nation-wide surveys of drug manufacture, distribution, promotion and prescription. It found that there were 'too many examples of companies which have marketed ineffective products, dangerous or even lethal products, atrociously over-promoted products or products that received government approval only on the basis of fraudulent evidence, and which were not punished in the market place'.[11]

The task force discovered that instead of prescribing in the way they had been taught in medical school, physicians were increasingly prescribing irrational combinations of drugs, drugs that were too risky for the trivial conditions for which they were recommended, and products that were all too likely to react adversely with each other.[12]

As remedial measures, the task force strongly advocated the use of a hospital formulary and prescription in generic names. Countering the drug industry's objections that a formulary would result in second-class health care and was an 'intolerable interference' with the right of physicians to prescribe as they saw fit, the task force maintained: 'In general, American physicians have found a formulary acceptable and practical, especially when it is designed by their clinical and scientific colleagues serving on expert committees, when quality is considered as important as price, when the formulary can be revised at appropriate intervals, and when there are provisions for prescribing unlisted drug products where special clinical conditions so demand. ... The use of a formulary is not a mark of second-class medicine but is, in fact, associated with the provision of the highest quality of medicine in the outstanding hospitals in the nation.'

Nearly a decade later, in 1976, eight out of the 25 most frequently prescribed drugs in the USA were found to be pharmacologically and therapeutically questionable.[13] In 1979, in the USA alone, one in every eight prescriptions (out of a total of 169 million) contained a drug considered ineffective according to the government's own standards. The cost to the nation of these ineffective drugs was US$1.1 billion.[14] The *Journal of the American Medical Association* wrote on 28 July 1994 that nearly six million elderly Americans are prescribed inappropriate and potentially hazardous drugs each year.[15]

A study in 1980 of prescriptions written by 72 general practitioners (GPs) in one area of England revealed that 42 per cent of these doctors had prescribed hazardous or undesirable drugs.[16]

Antihistamines are one example: on 8 April 1992, a US Congressional subcommittee was told by experts that Americans spend over US$1 billion every year on 'worthless, and possibly harmful' antihistamines, which are sold as common cold medicines.[17] Furthermore, Dr Richard Gorman of the Mary Poison Control Center informed the subcommittee that about 7 per cent of poisonings are related to medicines containing antihistamines. It has also been shown that antihistamine decongestant combinations provide no clinically significant relief in upper-respiratory-tract infections in children.[18]

Antidiarrhoeal drugs are also considered of dubious value. The *British Medical Journal* wrote in 1981: 'Appropriate treatment for the infant with gastroenteritis may be conveniently considered as the three Ds – drugs, dehydration, and diet. Drugs are mentioned only to discard them in most circumstances. Anti-emetics and intestinal sedatives are rarely effective and have definite side-effects.'[19] However, in the same year a survey in southwest England found that 30 per cent of patients with gastroenteritis were prescribed antidiarrhoeal drugs which did 'no good and [were] potentially harmful'.[20]

Also in 1981 in Britain, about 100,000 prescriptions for Lomotil (diphenoxylate hydrochloride) syrup were written for children. Lomotil is particularly unsuitable for younger children because it may be toxic at a dosage slightly higher than the therapeutic dose.[21] *The Rational Use of Drugs in the Management of Acute Diarrhoea in Children*, published by the World Health Organization (WHO), is testimony to the fact that the prescribing habits of physicians did not improve in the 1980s.[22] The *Lancet* wrote in 1991: 'Neither Diphenoxylate nor Loperamide can be recommended for use (against diarrhoea) in children, and there is thus no rationale for the production and sale of liquid and syrup formulations for paediatric use.'[23]

Dumping drugs on the Third World

If TNCs can continue to market drugs of doubtful efficacy in industrialised countries, one may imagine how easy it is for them to sell their products in countries with poor drug-regulatory machinery, high levels of illiteracy among consumers, and poor access to information on the part of the medical profession. In fact, there is widespread availability in the Third World of many drugs on the 'UN consolidated list of products whose consumption and/or sale have been banned, withdrawn, severely restricted or not approved by governments'. Some examples of these are given below:

Tonics An ordinary tonic, with 17 per cent alcohol content, marketed in the UK by Squibb as Verdiviton was promoted in India as a brain tonic. Between 1979 and 1984, six foreign companies occupied 49 per cent of the market in tonics with high-alcohol content in India. The lowest growth rate of these companies during this period was 47.2 per cent and the highest 108.9 per cent.[24]

Expectorants According to a 1983 report by the British National Formulary Committee, there is no scientific basis for the use of expectorants in the treatment of coughs and yet these are available and prescribed by doctors in the UK.[25] Between 1979 and 1984, five TNCs in India shared 52.9 per cent of the total market in expectorants. Sales of Piriton expectorant (chlorpheniramine maleate and ammonium chloride), manufactured by the British TNC, Glaxo, rose by 947 per cent during this period. Corex (chlorpheniramine, codeine phosphate and ephedrine), manufactured by Pfizer, achieved a 125.8 per cent growth rate, and the lowest growth rate of the five companies was 70.9 per cent.[26]

Cyproheptadine This drug is marketed in the UK by the US transnational Merck Sharp and Dohme for allergic rhinitis and various allergies under the brand name Periactin. The same product is marketed in India, Pakistan and other hunger-prone countries as an appetite stimulant.

Dipyrone (brand name Baralgan) was withdrawn by Hoechst from its country of origin, Germany, in 1987 because of serious side effects but continued to be marketed in most Third World countries. In India, dipyrone is among the top ten pharmaceutical products selling today.

Pentoxifylline (brand name Trental) is marketed in the UK and the USA by Hoechst for peripheral vascular diseases only. The same company is marketing Trental in the Third World for both peripheral and cerebral vascular problems and for the treatment of confused states of mind, loss of social contacts, sleeping disorders, vertigo and dizziness, loss of memory and loss of concentration.[27] The company has been very successful in confusing doctors and patients alike!

Meclizine hydrochloride Glaxo promotes this drug (brand name Ancoloxin) in the USA with the warning that the drug should not be prescribed to women who are or may be pregnant in view of its teratogenic effects on rats. In Britain, the data sheet for Ancoloxin states 'undesirable during first trimester of pregnancy ...

may be warranted if vomiting is severe'. However, in Africa (except South Africa) and Asia, Ancoloxin is promoted primarily for the treatment of 'nausea and vomiting during pregnancy'.[28]

Migril In marketing their products, TNCs not only make 'grossly exaggerated claims of efficacy and gloss over hazards'[29] but also in some cases increase the dosage in Third World countries. Burroughs Wellcome, a British TNC, recommended different doses in different countries of their product Migril (a combination of ergotamine tartrate, cyclizine hydrochloride, and caffeine hydrate) used for the treatment of migraine. The maximum weekly recommended dose was 10 mg in the USA, 12 mg in the UK and 24 mg in African and Asian countries.

Patents and compulsory licensing

Patents are an important means by which pharmaceutical companies are able to charge high prices. Most countries have a compulsory licensing provision in their patent act, through which some control is exercised over the prices charged, but the USA is an exception to this rule.

The British Patent Act of 1949 has two important sections. Section 41 allows the Comptroller of Patents to issue a compulsory licence for manufacture if the Comptroller considers that the patent monopoly is being misused. Section 46 enables the government to import a patented product from sources other than the patentee. In May 1961, the then health minister, Enoch Powell, invoked Section 46 of the Patent Act against US manufacturers to obtain cheaper supplies of tetracycline, chloramphenicol and chlorthiazide from Denmark and Italy for use in National Health Service (NHS) hospitals. Some years later, though, in 1975, the Conservative government in the UK actually extended patent life from 16 to 20 years.[30]

As a price-lowering measure, both the Kefauver Committee in the USA and the Sainsbury Committee in the UK had recommended reduction of patent life. After several years of investigations into the pricing and marketing practices of drug companies in the USA, Senator Kefauver introduced a bill in March 1962 to reduce exclusive patent rights from 17 years to three years: for the remaining 14 years, a patentee would be obliged to license the patent to other manufacturers for a royalty not exceeding 8 per cent of sales. But old-fashioned bribery worked. The bill did not go through. In the words of Ronald W. Lang: 'The drug industry lobby buys Congressmen's votes the way you and I buy aspirins.'[31]

An important amendment in the compulsory licensing provision of the Canadian Patent Act was approved by parliament in May 1964. Under this, a compulsory licence may be granted not only to manufacturers but also to importers to import drugs into Canada within the life of a patent. This was introduced to encourage price competition in the pharmaceuticals market.

Generic drugs versus brand-name drugs

Although generic drugs have been in existence since the 1890s, when they were mainly of naturally occurring and unpatented substances, it is only since the mid-1970s that the issue of generic drugs has gained a central position in the politics of pharmaceuticals.

A drug's generic name is the pharmacological name of the compound assigned either by WHO's International Non-proprietary Names Committee or by the US Adopted Name Council. Drugs whose patents have expired are also included in the category of generics.

Generic names help prescribers to think clearly about the therapeutic classification of drugs and are logical and scientific. They are used throughout doctors' training, but in both industrialised and Third World countries most doctors prescribe in brand names as a consequence of continuous and skilful promotion by the drug companies. In the absence of official information on drugs from the ministry of health or from medical institutions, doctors may succumb to glossy literature, free gifts and samples, and unrecorded fast sales talk. Frequent visits by sales representatives save doctors the trouble of reading medical journals and current textbooks. Brand images become imprinted in doctors' minds in such a way that they write them on prescriptions beyond patent protection years; consequently there is a strong monopolistic element which inhibits competition by similar products with generic or new brand names.[32]

Generic drugs are broadly classified into commodity generics and branded generics. Commodity generics, which have been on the market since the 1950s, are simply generic-name products marketed by a wide variety of companies. Branded generics, which are a more recent phenomenon, are either unpatented drugs sold under a brand name or patented or patent-expired products sold under a generic name prefixed by the company's initial(s) – a practice which helps differentiation from other generic manufacturers and is supposed to provide an assurance of quality. Branded generics are usually sold at a higher price than commodity generics.

The brand name of a drug is the trade-marked name, an integral part of the patent system. Together, brand names and patents insulate drug companies from price competition. For the same drug, there are a number of brand names in most countries: in the USA, an average of 30 names per drug. The drug industry conditions doctors so effectively that they often identify a drug only by a brand name.

Brand names do not necessarily guarantee quality. The Federal Drugs Administration found substandard drugs both in generic and brand-name products with about equal frequency.[33] Pfizer in the USA, Wellcome in the UK, and Hoffmann La Roche in Switzerland were found to be marketing defective batches of their brand-name products.[34] Quality assurance can only be guaranteed through stricter supervision by the drug-regulatory authority.

Claims by TNCs for the chemical superiority of brand-name drugs over generic products are often unjustified as the companies often buy either the bulk drug (raw materials) or the drug in its final dosage form from an identical source.

In the USA, ICN Pharmaceutical produces ampicillin for both the generic and brand divisions of Bristol Myers. It charges the brand-name section double the price paid by the generic division. During the early 1980s in Bangladesh, Albert David, a medium-sized public sector company, used to manufacture ampicillin and other antibiotics for Bristol Myers on a toll basis. (Toll manufacture is production by domestic companies on behalf of TNCs which do not have their own factories in a particular country.) Bristol Myers' brand of ampicillin (Pentrexyl), despite being twice the price of Albert David's own brand of ampicillin (Aldapen), sold better.

To undermine the generic industry in its infancy in the 1950s and 1960s, TNCs waged a strategic marketing war against low-cost generic-name products. Their vast army of sales representatives spread the rumour that generic drugs were produced by insanitary, incompetent and inexperienced cottage industries and that they were impure, contaminated or ineffective. They also waged their campaign through the pages of many medical journals and newsletters financed largely by drug advertising.[35] Moreover, they were able to enlist the leaders of the American Medical Association as their allies in their battle against small generic firms.[36]

The campaign of misinformation did not, however, lead to a decisive victory. A number of other factors combined to force a change of policy towards generics. The expiry dates of money-spinner patents started appearing on the horizon. New 'miracle drugs' were not in the offing because of a general decline in research productivity. Furthermore, the rising cost of health care was creating acute concern, especially among elderly people. Consumer groups, along with certain medical professionals, pharmacists, retired people and generics companies, became active in support of the increased use of generic drugs and demanded the repeal of the Anti-Substitution Law, enacted in 1952 to prevent retail pharmacists substituting generic drugs for prescribed brands without doctors' knowledge. Between 1971 and 1979, 47 states and the District of Columbia repealed or amended this law.

The Office of Pharmaceutical Reimbursement of the US Federal Government's Medicaid and Medicare programmes was similarly concerned about the rising cost of health care. In 1976, the Department of Health, Education and Welfare introduced the Maximum Allowable Cost Programme, which required Medicaid and Medicare recipients to limit reimbursement to certain multisource drugs available at the lowest price. Moreover, Medicare does not reimburse for drugs obtained outside hospitals.

TNCs bid for the generics market

By the mid-1960s, TNCs could see that their attempts to discredit generics were unlikely to succeed in the long term. The solution was to move in on the generics market themselves. In Britain, ICI introduced a branded-generic version of oxytetracycline in 1966 as soon as Pfizer's patent for the drug (brand name Terramycin) expired. In late 1971, SmithKline became the first company in the USA to introduce branded generics. Pfizer followed suit in 1972, creating a special generics division, Pfipharmces, and Lederle started marketing branded generics in 1976. Eli Lilly created its Dista division and started marketing both branded generics and commodity generics. In 1978, Boots and Glaxo acquired the generic-drugs companies Rucker and Meyer respectively. Most TNCs in the USA have now developed generics businesses either through the creation of a special division or by acquiring a generics company. Merck recently bought the generics company Medco for US$6.7 million.

In Germany, the BASF subsidiary Knoll acquired the leading generics company Hexal Pharma GMBH, whose annual turnover is DM 500 million. In the UK, Glaxo markets its branded generics through Duncan Flockart, and Fisons sells generics through Charnwood. Both Boots and Burroughs Wellcome have extensive branded-generic product lines. Berk is another well-known branded-generics company in the UK, which is owned by the US company United States Vitamin.

Cox and DDSA manufacture and market both types of generic drugs, while Cox is also a toll manufacturer for various TNCs. Hoechst acquired Cox in 1992 and created Cox (Japan) in 1994 to introduce generic drugs into Japan.[37] In anticipation of growing business, Glaxo established Evans Medical (New Zealand) in 1984 to produce branded generics in New Zealand. In 1979, Ciba-Geigy created Servipharm in order to enter the Third World generics market.

In June 1981 Gonoshasthaya Kendra (see p. xi) established Gonoshasthaya Pharmaceuticals Ltd (GPL) in order to manufacture and market low-priced branded generics in Bangladesh. GPL was the first company in Bangladesh to introduce branded generics.

The growth in generic drug prescriptions

Prescriptions of generic drugs are growing steadily in industrialised countries. Forty per cent of all US prescriptions in 1994 were for generic drugs,[38] compared with 9.2 per cent in 1974.[39] Sales of generics in New Zealand increased from 6 per cent in 1982 to 20 per cent in 1987.[40] In Britain, 47 per cent of prescriptions were written in generic names in 1993 and generic drugs were dispensed in 38 per cent of cases during the same period.[41]

How much cost-saving is possible through generic prescription? In 1994, the UK Audit Commission concluded that £84 million (US$126 million) would be saved annually if just 20 commonly used medicines were prescribed in generic names by every general practitioner in 50 selected practices (out of a total of 8,000 practices) in England and Wales.[42]

As both the number of generic prescriptions and the size of the generic-pharmaceuticals market grow steadily, will TNCs take over the generics market? According to Frank McKim, President of the US consultancy Scitec Services, if all the US research-based TNCs join the generics market, they are quite likely to dominate the market in the near future, although small independent generics manufacturers will remain as suppliers or toll manufacturers for TNCs.[43]

Research and development: an excuse for high drug prices

Drug prices continue to be beyond the reach of the common people. In 1993, US President Bill Clinton accused the drug companies of serious overpricing: 'Their profits are rising four times faster than the average *Fortune 500* company. And compared to other countries our prices are shocking ... . The drug industry spends one billion dollars more each year on advertising and lobbying than it does on developing new or better drugs.'[44] However, whereas in industrialised countries public finance and private insurance have cushioned consumers from the worst impact of high drug prices, in Third World countries consumers usually have to bear the expense themselves.

Transnational companies have justified prices as high as the market will tolerate, with claims of high research and development (R&D) costs. Yet, as Henry Waxman has rightly asserted in the US Congress, it is quite possible to have low drug prices and a thriving R&D-based pharmaceutical industry.[45]

Over the years, R&D spending, supposedly for the development of new drugs, has grown to unbelievable levels, from less than US$20 million in the 1970s to over US$30 billion in the 1990s. Even an 'insider' in the pharmaceutical industry, Professor Jurgen Drews, Head of R&D at Roche (Switzerland), has expressed the view that the industry is overspending on R&D.[46] Every year TNCs claim that they are increasing their investment in R&D. In 1992–93, 16 per cent of their turnover was purportedly spent on R&D (Table 1.2).

Table 1.2:   Sales of leading pharmaceutical companies and their R&D investment in 1992/93

Company and country	Sales (US$ million)	Change over previous year (percentage)	R&D expenditure (US$ million)	R&D expenditure (percentage of sales)
Merck & Co, USA	9,067.6	+13.7	1,057.5	11.7
Glaxo, UK	7,986.4	+10.8	1,197.1	15.0
Bristol Myers Squibb, USA	6,313.0	+ 6.9	934.0	14.8
Hoechst, Germany	6.042.1	+11.3	881.1	14.6
Ciba-Geigy, Switzerland	5,192.0	+12.6	711.1	15.5
SmithKlein & Beecham, UK	5,100.5	+16.7	727.4	14.8
Roche, Switzerland	4,896.0	+18.9	1,154.2	23.6
Sandoz, Switzerland	4,885.5	+10.0	793.6	16.2
Bayer, Germany	5,716.8	+ 8.4	794.6	13.9
Pfizer, USA	4,557.0	+20.9	863.0	18.9

Source: Thorpe, T., 'Leading companies in 1992/93' *Scrip Magazine*, London, January 1994.

In 1993, UK companies spent 50.5 per cent of their domestic sales (26.9 per cent of total sales including exports) on R&D. The number of research staff was 20,740: 25.8 per cent of the total staff employed in the industry.[47] According to the Association of British Pharmaceutical Industries, the UK pharmaceutical industry spends £4 million a day on R&D.[48]

However, closer examination of the situation casts real doubt on the claims made by TNCs about R&D and points to the fact that a very large proportion of the expenditure is for a wide range of costs other than those of genuine research. According to economist Sanjaya Lall,[49] research expenditure is extremely high because the research establishments are bigger than they need to be, a deliberate policy on the part of drug companies since R&D expenses are tax-deductible. As Moira Dower, editor of the pharmaceutical journal *Scrip*, has pointed out, 'how much it actually costs to research and develop a new drug is a matter of some debate'.[50]

Dr Sheldon Gilgore, Chief Executive Officer of Searle and the elected chairman of the US Pharmaceutical Manufacturers Association, commented in 1994: 'Britain does not have a thriving research-based pharmaceutical industry. In fact, it is just the opposite because of increasingly restrictive UK government policy.'[51]

Central costs usually include R&D administration at head office and regional-level offices staffed by marketing, business-planning, administration and research personnel. Money for clinical research is passed on to key medical figures engaged in pharmaceutical research. In Canada, 90 per cent of researchers foresaw a likely conflict of interest; 80 per cent deemed pharmaceutical clinical research to be 'me-too' research, while 75 per cent saw it as 'might-as-well' research; 40 per cent were worried about a potential delay in the publication of unfavourable results.[52]

Grants offered to physicians are included in research costs. Dr Sidney Wolfe, Director of the US Public Citizen Health Research Group, considers that in research grants, 'there is a spectrum of legitimate research on one end and research that is thinly disguised marketing on the other'.[53]

A breakdown of Hoechst's 1993 R&D expenditure of DM 1.6 billion provides some interesting insights.[54] (Table 1.3) It is obvious from the table that TNCs always incorporate a certain percentage of their expenditure on market development and marketing into R&D. Furthermore, pharmaceutical-company executives are the most overpaid personnel in all industries.[55]

High research costs are used as an argument for prolonging patent

Table 1.3:   R&D spending by Hoechst in 1993 according to therapeutic area, location of research, and type of R&D

Therapeutic area	Expenditure in 1993 (DM million)	Percentage of total expenditure
Cardiovascular	368	23
Behring Therapeutics	256	16
Metabolism	224	14
Anti-infective	176	11
Rheumatology	144	9
Hormones	128	8
Diagnostics	96	6
Neuro science	80	5
Genetic engineering/basic	32	2
Others	96	6
Total	1598	100

Location of research	Expenditure in 1993 (DM million)	Percentage of total expenditure
Germany	815	51
France	463	29
USA	176	11
Japan	112	7
Rest of world	32	2
Total	1598	100

Type of R&D	Expenditure in 1993 (DM million)	Percentage of total expenditure
Central costs	234	15
Clinical development*	507	32
Preclinical development*	228	14
Research costs*	215	13
Research projects	351	22
Others	63	4
Total	1598	100

* Including expenditure for market development and marketing of compounds.

Source: Hoechst refines R&D Strategy, *Scrip*, October 11, 1994.

rights for as long as 15 or 20 years. Patents protect monopolies and permit drug companies to make excessive profits, at the same time inhibiting competition in innovative research and encouraging imitative research. Projections of high research expenditure also deter smaller companies from embarking on research.

Few therapeutic gains, especially in the Third World

A US Senate inquiry found that out of 348 new drugs introduced by 25 large research-based pharmaceutical companies between 1981 and 1988, only twelve drugs (3.4 per cent) made an important therapeutic contribution; another 44 (12.6 per cent) were deemed to make a modest potential contribution, and the remaining 292 drugs (84 per cent) 'made little or no contribution'.[56] In 1988, 53 new chemical entities (NCEs) were introduced world-wide, of which only four were 'breakthrough' products.[57]

Of 39 NCEs introduced during 1993, ten were in the anti-infective therapeutic category, seven were for treatment of the central nervous system (three of these claimed to be effective in the improvement of memory and cognition), five were for cardiovascular conditions, five were anti-cancer products and the rest ranged from antidiarrhoeal products and lactation inhibitors to immuno-suppressants and products to prevent precocious puberty.[58] Twelve of the 39 NCEs were introduced by Japanese companies, eleven by US companies, five each by German and Swiss companies, three by French, two by Italian and one each by Danish, Norwegian, Austrian and Swedish companies. None was introduced by British companies.[59] In time we will know how many of these have brought genuine therapeutic gains. A guesstimate would be that the number will not reach double figures.

It is almost impossible to obtain reliable information on R&D investment. However, Canada is one country which seems to have reasonably reliable information on the subject. The Canadian Patent Act requires all companies with active Canadian patents to report their annual R&D expenditure. Eight out of 70 brand-name companies belonging to the Pharmaceutical Manufacturers Association of Canada reported no R&D expenditure in 1993. Of the remaining TNCs, those with sales of less than Canadian $30 million had spent 7.1 per cent of sales on R&D, while companies with sales of Canadian $90 million had spent 10.7 per cent of sales on R&D. In 1993, 60.3 per cent of patented pharmaceutical research in Canada was applied research, which consists largely of clinical and pre-clinical trials.[60]

If a 'knowledge plateau' has been reached in pharmaceutical research this is not primarily because of a depletion in research opportunities but because of lack of investment in basic research.[61] According to estimates by the Organization for Economic Co-operation and Development (OECD), basic pharmaceutical research world-wide absorbs 9.5 per cent of R&D costs.[62] In economic terms, the decline in true innovation means a decline in 'R&D productivity'.[63]

In India, TNCs' investment in R&D was about 0.8 per cent of their turnover in the 1980s, while that of the local pharmaceutical industry rose from 1.4 per cent in the 1970s to 2 per cent in the 1980s.[64] TNCs' R&D efforts have been restricted at best to process development, and hardly ever consist of formulation research.

It is estimated that US$30 billion was invested globally in health research in 1986, of which less than 5 per cent was specifically spent on Third World health problems.[65] According to a report published by the Association of British Pharmaceutical Industries, R&D is directed towards finding new therapies or improvements on existing treatments for diseases common in industrialised countries.[66] The search for cures for tropical diseases is not in the mainstream of pharmaceutical research. Just occasionally, drugs for tropical diseases emerge as by-products of veterinary medicine. The economic situation of Third World countries makes their people less attractive to TNCs than their animals and plants.

Promotion disguised as R&D

It is not genuine R&D expenditure but the cost of excessive and unethical promotion which increases drug prices.

It is estimated that the amount spent annually by the industry on each doctor in industrialised countries varies from US$2,665 in Canada, US$3,725 in Australia and US$3,065 in New Zealand, to around US$8,000 in the UK and the USA.[67]

Advertising is an integral part of a market economy. But what about the quality of advertising? Research on newspaper and magazine advertisements for over-the-counter drugs in eleven countries (Germany, Denmark, The Netherlands, the UK, Australia, Switzerland, Israel, New Zealand, Sweden, Finland and the USA) showed that only three out of 183 advertisements met all the criteria of the European Union's Directive on Advertising of Medical Products (1992) and WHO's Ethical Criteria for Medicinal Drug Promotion (1988).[68] The average number of breaches of these codes per advertisement was 4.6, mostly consisting of failure to mention contra-indications or warn of side-effects. The three advertisements which fulfilled the obligations had printed the information about contra-indications and side-effects in such small type that nobody would have been able to read it with any ease.

A European Union (EU) Council Directive of 31 March 1992 clearly states that advertisements 'shall encourage the rational use of the medical product, representing it objectively and without exagger-ating its properties' and that they 'shall not be misleading'.[69]

Promotion and advertising costs in the USA are said to be three to four times the costs of R&D. In India, TNCs' marketing and allied costs amount to about 33 per cent,[70] which is similar to the promotion costs in industrialised countries. In 1989, every French GP received on average 160 kg of unsolicited promotional materials.[71] British GPs were no less fortunate. In 1983, each received a monthly average of over 45 kg of advertising literature and assorted free gifts including notepads, diaries, pens and records which prominently displayed the brand names of drugs.[72] In Bangladesh, certain busy female doctors receive expensive gold necklaces.[73]

In November 1988, at an estimated cost of over US$100,000, Ciba-Geigy brought 150 US doctors and their partners to a weekend meeting in an island resort off Florida to discuss its non-steroidal anti-inflammatory drug Volteran (diclofenac).[74] Other well-known promotional practices employed by TNCs include the holding of drug symposia in leading French ski resorts, meetings-cum-golf tournaments, and weekend symposia followed by visits to a motor race or the opera in Paris.[75]

It is obvious that these promotional activities create a demand far greater than actual needs.[76] Dr Halfdan Mahler, Director-General of the World Health Organization (1973–1988), often expressed his dismay at the 'double standards of the drug industry's marketing practices' and reminded the industry of its 'global social respons-ibility for the availability of essential drugs'.[77] But the drug industry remained unrepentant. According to the US Pharmaceutical Manufacturers Association, '[most] of the US industry has little to apologize for in the realm of social responsibility and in the pharma-ceutical industry least of all'.[78]

Transfer pricing

The term 'transfer pricing' is never mentioned in textbooks on medicine or pharmacology. Practised in both industrialised and

Third World countries, transfer pricing has been defined as a method of financial manipulation 'to shift profits clandestinely from one area of operation to another' with a view to depriving the governments of both the host country and the TNC's home country of legitimate tax revenue.[79] Commonly, the practice involves the overpricing of imports, including inflation of the initial value of capital equipment. TNCs often transfer their old equipment (with nil book value) from one Third World country to another where they record the current market price of the equipment (or even more) through a system of over-invoicing. By such deceptive techniques, TNCs show high investment and expenditure in both countries. Pfizer (Bangladesh) for example, imported most of its machinery from its factory in India. Transfer pricing also involves collusion with local partners 'to provide funds for accumulation abroad or for resale on the black market'.[80]

During the 1960s, the US company Eaton was charging the British NHS 102 times more for nitrofurantoin than it was charging some other customers, while ICI was charging the NHS 60 times more for propranolol, and SmithKline was charging 145 times more for trifluoperazine.[81]

In 1973, the UK Monopolies Commission found that between 1966 and 1972 Roche (UK) had been purchasing active ingredients for the brands Librium (chlordiazepoxide) and Valium (diazepam) at £370 and £972 per kg from the Swiss parent company Hoffman La Roche.[82] The same ingredients were available at £9 and £20 per kg respectively in Italy. The commission calculated that during this period Roche's profit on capital employed was not 5 per cent, as declared by the company, but over 70 per cent. Roche sold Librium at different prices in different parts of the USA, as well as at different prices in different countries.[83]

In 1968, a team led by the economist Constantine Vaitsos was asked by the Colombian Government to solve the riddle of why the transnational companies, which were reporting around 6 per cent profit, much lower than the country's inflation rate, were nevertheless seeking to expand their production facilities.[84] Vaitsos and his team undertook a careful examination, over a period of eleven months, of all the customs documents relating to 1,500 imported intermediate products. They discovered that the transnational corporations were in reality making a profit of 79 per cent and that Roche was overpricing diazepam/Valium and chlordiazepoxide/Librium by 6,155 per cent and 6,478 per cent respectively. The prices charged by Roche (UK) for these two drugs in the mid-1970s to two Third

Table 1.4:   Roche wholesale prices of Librium (chlordiazepoxide) and Valium (diazepam) in selected countries in 1975 in US$

Country	Price of 100 capsules of Librium (US$)	Percentage of UK price of Librium	Price of 100 tablets of Valium (US$)	Percentage of UK price of Valium
United Kingdom (UK)	0.83	100	0.63	100
Germany	4.38	528	5.35	849
Switzerland	4.75	572	5.44	908
USA	5.80	699	6.89	1093
Mexico*	4.42	532	6.03	957
Costa Rica*	7.03	847	9.13	1449

*Data for 1976.

Source: Gereffi, G., *The Pharmaceutical Industry and Dependency in the Third World*, Princeton University Press, Princeton, 1983.

World and three industrialised countries were between eight and 14 times the UK price (Table 1.4).

A study conducted by the United Nations Economic and Social Council found that the steroid hormone oestradiol, extracted from barbasco, a Mexican medicinal plant, by a local firm named Syntex was exported in 1972 at US$880 per kg, while the same product was imported into Mexico in the same year by a TNC at US$80,000 per kg. Similarly, progesterone was exported from Mexico at US$110 per kg and imported by Mexico in 1972 at US$2,490 per kg.[85]

In 1961, Pfizer was charging the British NHS US$64 for 1,000 capsules of the antibiotic tetracycline, which it sold to Holland and France for US$28.[86] In the early 1970s, tetracycline was sold in Europe for US$24–30 per kg, while drugs containing the same ingredients were sold to India, Pakistan and Colombia for between US$100 and US$270 per kg.[87] In 1980, the cheapest brand of tetracycline cost eight times more in the Philippines than in the USA, while the same capsule was sold in Malaysia (which has a better regulatory apparatus than the Philippines) at double the US price.[88]

Between July 1979 and June 1980, Squibb (Bangladesh) imported tetracycline at three times the price paid by local companies. The director of the Drug Administration issued a warning to the company as their cost and freight price of tetracycline was much higher than that of other competitive sources.[89] During the same period, Bangladesh Pharmaceutical Industry (BPI), a joint venture of Rhone Poulenc of France and the Bangladesh Government, imported metronidazole at five times the price paid by other local manufacturers. In 1979, a report by the World Bank had also commented: 'The relatively very high cost of some medicines produced commercially in Bangladesh is striking.'[90]

Doctors' lack of knowledge

Every commodity has a use value and an exchange value. Doctors and patients view drugs as a means to fight disease and ameliorate suffering. But to their producers, drugs are commodities. Drug companies are concerned less with the usefulness of a drug, or whether or not it has serious side-effects, than with obtaining the highest possible exchange value for it.

Doctors often fail to appreciate that pharmaceutical companies are driven by commercial interests. This is not surprising since the economics of drug production and health care, the marketing strategies of drug manufacturers, high drug prices and the issue of affordability are not part of medical education in either industrialised or Third World countries.

Doctors become very agitated at any hint of infringement of their 'clinical freedom'. Yet, freedom of choice is only possible with appropriate knowledge, and knowledge depends on access to information and the time and skill to find a way through the maze of different brands.[91] How many doctors in the world have this kind of knowledge? Even in industrialised countries most doctors are unaware of the important reports on the drug industry and its unethical practices that have been produced periodically over the decades. These include Senator Kefauver's report to the US Senate,[92] the Sainsbury Committee's report to the British House of Commons,[93] two reports by the United Nations Conference on Trade and Development (UNCTAD)[94] and one by the United Nations Commission on Transnational Corporations.[95] Doctors in the Third World have even less access to such information. The Kefauver and Sainsbury reports were not even mentioned either in the news media or in the medical journals of the then East Pakistan (now Bangladesh) in the 1960s and 1970s.

Although the patient is the apparent purchaser of a drug, the choice of the drug is made by the doctor. That is why so much promotion by drug companies is geared towards doctors. Doctors often have no knowledge of the pharmaceuticals market, especially of price variations between similar or identical drugs manufactured by different companies and marketed under different brand names. This kind of information is not provided by ministries of health; nor is it automatically a part of doctors' education. Departments of clinical pharmacology, where such topics are taught, are almost non-existent in the medical schools of Third World countries and are not fully developed in all medical schools in industrialised countries. Drug companies are fully aware of the fact that doctors lack knowledge about prices and, where there is little or no market regulation by the government, drugs are sold at much higher prices. In the Third World, doctors are totally dependent on the information given by drug companies. Besides, they have not been taught to be concerned about the cost-effectiveness of treatment. Both medical practitioners and consumers tend to have a rigid faith in the quality of high-priced imported drugs, which are considered more effective than locally produced ones and can also be seen as a status symbol.[96]

Thus doctors are the least equipped to discern the validity of drug-company promotions, yet decisions regarding the choice of drugs remain firmly in their hands. That is why they are prone to bad prescribing habits.

In 1987, researchers at Cambridge Hospital (USA) and Harvard Medical School found that about 80 per cent of Americans over the age of 65 were receiving at least one contra-indicated drug while the remaining 20 per cent were receiving two or more contra-indicated drugs. The researchers also observed that the costly newer drugs prescribed '[did] not represent an improvement in drug therapy over older, less expensive agents with proven records of safety and effectiveness'.[97]

The *British Medical Journal* wrote in October 1994 that adequate, correct information about drugs and greater openness generally would 'help family doctors prescribe more rationally and cheaply, reduce the yearly toll of 240,000 admissions to hospitals because of drug reactions and save some 150 tonnes of medicines thrown away each year by uninformed patients'.[98]

The situation in Third World countries is many times worse.

Notes

1. Thorpe, Tracey, 'Leading companies 1992/1993', *Scrip Magazine*, London, January 1994.

2. Ibid.

3. Braithwaite, John, *Corporate Crime in the Pharmaceutical Industry*, Routledge and Kegan Paul, 1983.

4. 'Essential Drugs: A Concept in Action', *HAI News*, Penang, April 1988.

5. Silverman, M., Lee, P. R. and Lydecker, M., *Prescriptions for Death: The Drugging of the Third World*, University of California Press, Berkeley, 1982.

6. 'Special Report and First and Second Reports of the Committee of Public Accounts', Session 1959–60, HMSO, London, quoted in Lang, R. W., *The Politics of Drugs: The British and Canadian Pharmaceutical Industries and Governments – A Comparative Study*, Saxon House/Lexington Books, Lexington, USA, 1974.

7. Sainsbury Committee, *Report of the Committee of Enquiry into the Relationship of the Pharmaceutical Industry with the National Health Services, 1965–67*, HMSO, London, 1967.

8. Medawar, C., *The Wrong Kind of Medicine?*, Social Audit, London, 1984.

9. Hathi Committee, 'Report of the Committee on the Drugs and Pharmaceutical Industry', Ministry of Petroleum and Chemicals, Government of India, New Delhi, April 1975.

10. US Department of Health, Education and Welfare, Office of the Secretary, *Task Force on Prescription Drugs*, US Government Printing Office, Washington DC, 1969, quoted in Silverman, M., Lydecker, M. and Lee, P. R., *Bad Medicine: The Prescription Drug Industry in the Third World*, Stanford University Press, California, 1992.

11. Silverman, M., Lee, P. R. and Lydecker, M., *Prescriptions for Death: The Drugging of the Third World*, op. cit.

12. Silverman, M., Lydecker, M. and Lee, P. R., *Bad Medicine: The Prescription Drug Industry in the Third World*, Stanford University Press, California, 1992.

13. Knapp, D. E., 'Can pharmacists influence drug prescribing?', *American Journal of Hospital Pharmacy*, Vol. 35, No. 593, 1978, quoted in Medawar, C., *The Wrong Kind of Medicine?*, op. cit.

14. Wolfe, S. M., Coley, C. M. and Health Research Group, *Pills That Don't Work*, Farrar Strauss Giroux, New York, 1981.

15. *Journal of the American Medical Association*, 28 July 1994, quoted in 'Wrong drugs prescribed for elderly', *Scrip*, London, 9 August 1994.

16. Catford, J., 'Quality of prescribing for children in general practice', in *British Medical Journal*, London, 14 June, 1980.

17. 'USA: Antihistamines in cold remedies', *The Lancet*, 25 April 1992.

18. Blake, K. D., 'Dangers of common cold treatments in children', *The Lancet*, London, 6 March 1993.

19. Wharton, B. A., 'Gastroenteritis in Britain: management at home', (editorial), *British Medical Journal*, London, 14 November 1981.

20. Morrison P. S. and Little, T. M., 'How is gastroenteritis treated?', *British Medical Journal*, London, 14 November 1981.

21. Medawar, C., *The Wrong Kind of Medicine?*, op. cit.

22. *The Rational Use of Drugs in the Management of Acute Diarrhoea in Children*, World Health Organization, 1990.

23. 'Anti-diarrhoeal drugs (not) for children', *The Lancet*, 19 January 1991.

24. Guha, Amitava, 'Marketing of Medicine: Parasitology of Profit' in *Drug Industry and Indian People*, Gupta, Amit Sen (ed), FMRAI/Delhi Science Forum, New Delhi, 1986.

25. *British National Formulary*, No. 6, British Medical Association/Pharmaceutical Society of Great Britain, London, 1983.

26. Guha, Amitava, op. cit.

27. Silverman, M., Lydecker, M. and Lee, P. R., *Bad Medicine: The Prescription Drug Industry in the Third World*, op. cit.

28. Medawar, C., Insult or Injury? *An Enquiry into the Marketing and Advertising of British Food and Drug Products in the Third World*, Social Audit, London, 1979.

29. Silverman, M., Lee, P.R. and Lydecker, M., 'Drug Promotion: The Third World Revisited', *International Journal of Health Services*, Vol.16, No. 4, Baltimore, 1986.

30. *Patent Law Reform*, HMSO, London, 1975.

31. Lang, R. W., *The Politics of Drugs: The British and Canadian Pharmaceutical Industries and Governments – A Comparative Study*, Saxon House/Lexington Books, Lexington, USA, 1974.

32. Lall, Sanjaya, *The Multinational Corporation*, Macmillan, London, 1980.

33. Simmons, H. E., article in the *Journal of the American Pharmaceutical Association*, Vol. 13, No. 96, 1973, quoted in Bibile, S./UNCTAD, *Case Sudies in Transfer of Technology: Pharmaceutical Policies in Sri Lanka*, UNCTAD Secretariat, United Nations, Geneva, June 1977.

34. John Yudkin, personal communications to Milton Silverman in 1980 and 1981, quoted in Silverman, M., Lee, P. R. and Lydecker, M., *Prescriptions for Death: The Drugging of the Third World*, op. cit.

35. Silverman, M., Lydecker, M. and Lee, P. R., *Bad Medicine: The Prescription Drug Industry in the Third World*, op. cit.

36. Silverman, M., Lee, P. R. and Lydecker, M., *Prescriptions for Death: The Drugging of the Third World*, op. cit.

37. 'Hoechst generic initiative in Japan', *Scrip*, London, 6 December 1994.

38. 'Generic savings for US consumers', *Scrip*, London, 14 October 1994.

39. WHO, *The World Drug Situation*, World Health Organization, Geneva, 1988.

40. Davis, Peter (ed), *For Health or Profit: Medicine, the Pharmaceutical Industry and the State in New Zealand*, Oxford University Press, Auckland, 1991.

41. 'English script cost up', *Scrip*, London, 5 August 1994.

42. UK Audit Commission, 'A prescription for improvement: Towards more rational prescribing in General Practice', quoted in '£425 million savings from more rational prescribing', *Scrip*, London, 11 March 1994. The commonly used brand-name drugs were: Tagamet (cimetidine), Lasix (frusomide), Tenormin (atenolol), Inderal (propranolol), Trandate (labetalol), Aldactone (spironolactone), Trasicor (oxprenolol), Aldomet (methyldopa), Ventolin (salbutamol), Maxolon (metoclopramide), Floxapen (flucloxacillin), Amoxil (amoxicillin), Erythropaed/Erythrocin (erythromycin), Septrin (cotrimexazole), Flazyl (metronidazole), Daonil (glibenclamide), Brufen (ibobrufen), Naprosyn (naproxen), Feldene (piroxicam) and Zyloric (allopurinol).

43. 'PMA firms to dominate US generics?', *Scrip*, London, 10 August 1994.

44. US President Bill Clinton's speech in Arlington (Virginia), reported by Agence France Presse on 13 February 1993 and quoted in 'Clinton accuses drug industry of overpricing vaccines', *Bangladesh Observer*, Dhaka, 15 February 1993. A 'Fortune 500' company is one listed by *Fortune* magazine in its annual list of the top 500 companies.

45. 'UK now less innovative, say UK firms', *Scrip*, London, 15 February 1994.

46. 'Industry overspending on R&D', *Scrip*, London, 5 October 1993.

47. 'European pharma R&D spend in 1993', *Scrip*, London, 13 September 1994.

48. 'ABPI stresses inward investment priority', *Scrip*, London, 23 August 1994.

49. Lall, Sanjaya, *The Multinational Corporation*, op. cit.

50. Dower, Moria, 'Managing the "D" in R&D', *Scrip Magazine*, London, July-August 1994.

51. 'UK no longer a force in innovation, say US companies', *Scrip*, London, 15 February 1994.

52. Taylor, K. M., 'The impact of the pharmaceutical industry's clinical research programs on medical education, practice and researchers in Canada: a discussion paper in Canadian pharmaceutical research and development', Ottawa, 1991, quoted in Lexchin, Joel, *Pharmaceuticals, Patents and Policies: Canada and Bill C-22*, The Canadian Centre for Policy Alternatives, Ottawa, February 1992.

53. 'Bribing of US doctors continuing', *Scrip*, London, 23 September 1994.

54. 'Hoechst refines R&D strategy', *Scrip*, London, 11 October 1994.

55. 'Overpaid UK pharma executives', *Scrip*, London, 14 October 1994.

56. Marsh, P., 'Prescribing all the way to the bank', *New Scientist*, London, 18 November 1989.

57. Ibid.

58. Davies, J., 'New Chemical Entities for unmet medical needs', *Scrip Magazine*, London, January 1994.

59. Ibid.

60. 'Canadian patented pharma R&D review', *Scrip*, London, 29 July 1994.

61. United Nations Centre on Transnational Corporations, *Transnational Corporations and the Pharmaceutical Industry*, United Nations, New York, 1979.

62. Burstall, M. L., Dunning, J. H. and Lake, A., 'Multinational Enterprises, Governments and Technology: Pharmaceutical Industry', OECD, Paris, 1981, quoted in Chetley, A., *A Healthy Business? World Health and the Pharmaceutical Industry*, Zed Books, London/New Jersey, 1990.

63. UNCTC, Transnational Corporations and the Pharmaceutical Industry, United Nations, New York, 1979.

64. Mehrotra, N. N., 'R&D and Technological Development in Indian Drug Industry Policy: Perspectives, Problems and Prospects' in Ekbal, B. (ed), *A Decade After the Hathi Committee*, KSSP, Kerala, India, May 1988.

65. Commission on Health Research for Development, *Health Research: Essential Link to Equity in Development*, Oxford University Press, Oxford, 1990.

66. Maddox, John, *Pharmaceutical Research and Public Ownership*, Association of the British Pharmaceutical Industry, London, March 1975.

67. Chetley, A. and Mintzes, B. (eds), *Promoting Health or Pushing Drugs?*, Health Action International (HAI-Europe), Amsterdam, 1992.

68. Kaldeway, H., Wieringa, N., Herxheimer, A. and Vos, R., 'A searching look at advertisements: A content analysis of magazine and newspaper advertisements for OTC medicines and health products in 11 countries', International Organisation of Consumers Unions, London, August 1994.

69. EU Council Directive 92/28/EEC.

70. Mehrotra, N. N., op. cit.

71. '160 kg of French promotion per GP practice', *Scrip*, London, 6 June 1990.

72. Bennett, C., 'The remedy of drugs', *Marketing Week*, 8 June 1984, quoted in *Promoting Health or Pushing Drugs?*, Chetley, A. and Mintzes, B. (eds), op. cit.

73. Rolt, Frances, *Pills, Policies and Profits*, War on Want, London, 1985.

74. Chetley, A. and Mintzes, B. (eds), *Promoting Health or Pushing Drugs?*, op. cit.

75. Ibid.

76. WHO, *The Selection of Essential Drugs*, TRS 615, World Health Organization, Geneva, 1977.

77. Mahler, H., 'Prophylactic and Therapeutic Substances', Report of the Director General, 28th World Health Assembly, Geneva, 3 April 1975.

78. Baskin, Claudia, *PMA Newsletter*, March 1981, quoted in Silverman M. et al., *Prescriptions for Death: The Drugging of the Third World*, op. cit.

79. Lall, Sanjaya and Streeten, Paul, *Foreign Investment, Transnationals and Developing Countries*, Macmillan, London, 1977.

80. Lall, Sanjaya, *The Multinational Corporation*, op. cit.

81. 'Do all drugs cost too much?', *Sunday Times*, London, 27 May 1973, quoted in Lall, Sanjaya, *The Multinational Corporation*, op. cit.

82. The Monopolies Commission, *A Report on the Supply of Chlordiazepoxide and Diazepam*, HMSO, London, 1973.

83. Lall, Sanjaya, *The Multinational Corporation*, op. cit.

84. C. V. Vaitsos, 'Patents Revisited: Their Functions in Developing Countries', in *Science Technology and Development*, Cooper, C. (ed), Frank Cass, 1973.

85. 'Transnational Corporations in the Pharmaceutical Industry of Developing Countries', E/C 10/85, United Nations Economic and Social Council, New York, 1981.

86. Lang, R.W., op. cit.

87. 'Near-Criminal Drug Prices in Backward Countries', *Guardian*, London, 6 September 1973, quoted in *Who Needs the Drug Companies*, Haslemere Group/War on Want, London, 1976.

88. Batista, Esteban and Clemente, Wilfredo with UNCTAD, 'Technology Policies in the Pharmaceutical Sector in the Philippines', UNCTAD, United Nations, Geneva, 1980, quoted in Tiranti, D. J., *Essential Drugs: The Bangladesh Experience Four Years On*, IOCU/New Internationalist Publications/War on Want, London, 1986.

89. Anwar M. Nurul, Director, Drug Administration, letter to Squibb (Bangladesh) regarding approval of master file (Block List) for tetracycline HCl, Dhaka Letter No. DAP/ARP-42, 13 November 1982.

90. *Procurement and Manufacture of Drugs for Use in PHC in Bangladesh*, World Bank Study Team Report, Dhaka, May 1979.

91. Collier, J., *The Health Conspiracy*, Century, London, 1989.

92. US Senate, Committee on the Judiciary, Subcommittee on Anti-Trust and Monopoly, *Administered Prices in the Drug Industry 1959–62*, US Government Printing, Washington D.C., 1965. This committee was chaired by Senator Kefauver and thus became known as the Kefauver Committee.

93. Sainsbury Committee, op. cit.

94. UNCTAD, *Major Issues in the Transfer of Technology to Developing Countries: A Case Study of the Pharmaceutical Industry*, UNCTAD Secretariat, United Nations, Geneva, 1975 and *Trade Marks and Generic Names of Pharmaceuticals and Consumer Protection*, UNCTAD Secretariat, United Nations, 1981.

95. UNCTC, *Transnational Corporations and the Pharmaceutical Industry*, op. cit.

96. Agarwal, P. S., Ramchandran, P. K. and Rangarao, B. V., 'Anomalies in Drug Prices and Quality Control', *Economic and Political Weekly*, Bombay, 18 November 1972.

97. 'Wrong drugs prescribed for elderly', *Scrip*, London, 9 August 1994.

98. 'Stop drug secrecy, says government watch dog', *British Medical Journal*, London, 1 October 1994.

2

Reform attempts

The gravity of the situation in the global market clearly called for the introduction of regulations in the pharmaceutical sector, especially in Third World countries. The 1970s saw a number of significant developments that combined to create an atmosphere of confidence in the capacity of the Third World to make bold and independent decisions which could improve the lives of its peoples:

- In 1973, the decision by the Organisation of Petroleum Exporting Countries (OPEC) to increase the price of oil, although leading to a global oil crisis, brought about a renewed awareness of the exploitation of the South in terms of the ridiculously low prices paid for its raw materials. The OPEC stance transmitted a feeling of empowerment among Third World countries.
- On 18 May 1974, India detonated its first nuclear bomb, a 15 kiloton plutonium device. This event was of considerable symbolic significance as it indicated that a Third World country was capable of becoming a nuclear power and of resisting Western domination.
- The fall of Saigon and the military defeat of the USA at the hands of the Socialist Republic of Vietnam in 1976 was seen as the victory of a Third World people against a First World super-power and led to calls for pro-people policy reforms in Afro-Asia, especially in South and Southeast Asia.
- The Non-Aligned Movement (NAM) also gained in strength and importance during this period, with India taking a particularly active role. Pakistan, though not a part of NAM, developed a strong friendship with China. New alliances began to be formed that offered the possibility of reducing the Third World's dependence on the industrialised powers of the North.

It was during the 1970s that attempts by a number of Third World countries to introduce reforms in the pharmaceuticals sector gathered momentum. These reforms invariably met with strong opposition and most were swiftly undermined or defeated. Nevertheless, the initiatives had a cumulative effect, encouraging international movements and organisations such as the Non-Aligned Movement and the World Health Organization to formulate policies on drugs, and paving the way for other countries to take action in the 1980s and 1990s.

Reform of India's patent laws

In its Patents Act of 1970, India ushered in a change affecting the lives of millions of its citizens.[1] Before this, over 80 per cent of all patents and 95 per cent of pharmaceutical patents had been held by foreigners (Tables 2.1 and 2.2). A similar situation prevailed in Canada. The Report of the Commission of Patents for Canada for

Table 2.1: Patents held by Indians and foreigners in India 1856–1970

Year	Patent applications by Indians (number)	(percentage)	Patent applications by foreigners (number)	(percentage)
1856	0	Nil	33	100
1900	44	9	448	91
1920	99	19	938	90
1940	213	29	528	71
1947	220	9	2,150	91
1960	662	15	3,841	85
1970	1,116	22	4,026	78

Source: Keyala, B.K., *Patents Regime: Indian Experience and Options Available*, National Working Group on Patent Laws, New Delhi, 1992.

Table 2.2: Patent applications for vital industries in India 1947–57

Type of industry	Number of patent applications	Patent application by Indians (number)	(percentage)	Patent applications by foreigners (number)	(percentage)
Food	1,850	222	12	1,628	88
Chemicals	3,717	311	8	3,406	92
Pharmaceuticals	3,035	143	5	2,892	95

Source: Keyala B.K., *Patents Regime: Indian Experience and Options Available*. National Working Group on Patent Laws, New Delhi, 1992.

the year ending 31 March 1963 showed that, out of a total of 22,014 patents issued, only 2,036 (9.2 per cent) were held by Canadian citizens or companies. In the case of drug patents, less than 5 per cent were held by Canadians.[2] In Britain, in 1963, Swiss drug companies alone held 30 per cent of all drug patents, while British subjects held 47 per cent.[3]

In India, foreign companies enjoyed a virtual monopoly and most goods were imported at extremely high prices. India paid US$10 per kg for vitamin C while Europe and the USA paid US$2.40. A survey of eight common drugs showed an average price increase of 42 per cent between 1967 and 1970.[4]

Under the Indian Patents Act, the process of manufacture of a substance to be used as food or medicine can be patented for five years from the date of sealing of the patent or seven years from the date of patent application. Unlike the US and UK patent laws, the Indian law prohibits product patenting for food and medicine. Patents for any other inventions are valid for 14 years. The government retains the right to cancel or revoke already granted patent licences in the public interest and to import and distribute patented drugs for public and private sector use.

Through this reform, the national interest was given priority over the interests of the patentee. As a result, indigenous drug production grew very fast. Indian scientists and technologists developed over 100 innovative processes for important bulk drugs such as antibiotics, steroids and vitamins, and drugs for treating cardiac diseases, ulcers and cancer.

Sri Lanka: the pioneer in drug regulation

Ruled consecutively by the Portuguese, Dutch and British for 150 years each, Sri Lanka gained its independence from British rule in 1947. After independence, public sector health services expanded vastly all over the country, as did education and social welfare. Private medicine also grew steadily.

A fast-growing problem with which public sector medicine had to contend was that of the proliferation of brand names of the same generic drug. Procurement and store-keeping became an almost impossible task. To tackle the problem, the then Health Minister appointed a Formulary Committee in 1958, chaired by Professor Senaka Bibile of the University of Colombo. The other members of the committee were two consultant physicians, a paediatrician and a surgeon. In April 1959, the committee prepared the Ceylon

Hospitals Formulary, listing around 500 drugs in their generic names and explaining their pharmacology and use.[5] This was the second-earliest hospital formulary in the Third World, the first being in Chile. Public hospitals were obliged to restrict their prescription to drugs listed in the formulary.

A severe balance-of-payments crisis in 1962 forced the health ministry to ask the formulary committee (under the new name of the National Formulary Committee, or NFC) to review the usefulness of the 4,000 imported drugs that were in use in the private sector. The NFC's recommendations, published in 1963, included restriction of drug importation to just 2,100 approved drugs. Unfortunately, the government did not impose any limit on the number of brands per approved drug or any restrictions on their promotion. Even so, the adoption of an approved list of drugs for the private sector was a significant step.

The NFC started a quarterly publication, *Formulary Notes*, in 1966 to provide current information on drugs to medical practitioners. In 1968, the government introduced price controls, limiting the retail price of a drug to no more than twice the price of importing it. Unfortunately, this attempt was unsuccessful because manufacturers and importers managed to inflate the price of imports.

In the early 1970s, Sri Lanka led the way in the economic procurement of essential drugs and succeeded in reducing prices through bulk purchase. Sri Lanka's experience also unmasked the symbiotic relationship between the drug companies and the doctors and demonstrated the way in which transnationals, backed by their governments, especially the US, are able to exert considerable pressure on Third World countries.

Following a landslide electoral victory in May 1970, a coalition government was formed under the leadership of Mrs Sirimavo Bandaranaike of the Sri Lanka Freedom Party, who became the first female prime minister in the world. Her government changed the name of the country from Ceylon to Sri Lanka, its original name before colonial rule. Dr N. M. Perera of the Sri Lanka Communist Party was appointed Finance Minister, while T. B. Subasinghe of the Sri Lanka Sama (Socialist) Samaj Party was made Minister for Industries and Scientific Affairs. These two men played important roles in the implementation of a rational pharmaceutical policy in Sri Lanka.

In October 1970, the coalition government asked Professor Senaka Bibile and Dr S. A. Wickremasinghe, the leader of the Sri Lanka Communist Party and a practising family physician in a small town in the south of the island, to investigate and report on the situation of the pharmaceutical industry in Sri Lanka.

They found that the subsidiaries of three British TNCs (Glaxo, Reckitt & Colman, and Burroughs Wellcome represented by UNICAL) and two US companies (Pfizer and Warner-Hudnut) accounted for 75 per cent of local production. Two local companies under licence from transnationals controlled another 22 per cent, and the remaining 3 per cent of production was in the hands of seven small local companies. Furthermore, drugs were freely imported from abroad. Over 800 health centres and government hospitals were supplied by the State Medical Stores (SMS), and the private sector was supplied by 134 local agents of foreign companies. Several thousand brands of 2,100 drugs, mostly imported, were available on the market and many of these were ineffective, unnecessarily expensive or irrational combinations. The Bibile-Wickremasinghe report[6] was submitted to the Prime Minister on 21 March 1971 and made the following recommendations:

- All imports of finished products and bulk drugs (i.e. pharmaceutical chemicals and active ingredients) should be channelled through a State Trading Corporation, which would ensure quality imports from the cheapest possible sources.
- The patent law should be amended, product patents abolished, the number of imported drugs reduced and only rationally formulated drugs imported.
- Brand names should be replaced by generic names in the sale and prescription of drugs. Promotion by drug companies should be prohibited and information on drugs should be provided by the government only, through the NFC's *Formulary Notes* (renamed *The Prescriber* in 1973).
- Local manufacturers, both foreign and national, should produce drugs according to a Rationalised Drug List, using the ingredients imported by the State Trading Corporation. In the case of non-compliance, the company should be nationalised under the Sri Lanka State Trading Corporation (Drugs) Act.

Recommendations also included the training of pharmacists, improvement of quality control procedures, reorganisation of the SMS and importation from cheaper sources in Eastern Europe. On 21 September 1971, the State Pharmaceuticals Corporation (SPC) was established, with Professor Bibile as its chairman. Its broad functions were announced in the *Government Gazette*:[7]

- the import, export, purchase, sale and distribution of drugs;
- the purchase, sale and distribution of locally manufactured or processed drugs;
- the manufacture, processing, stocking, packing and repacking of drugs;
- coordination, promotion, development and rationalisation of the manufacture and processing of drugs;
- provision of technical assistance for the manufacture and processing of drugs;
- pharmacological and pharmaceutical research and the standardisation of drugs;
- the quality control of drugs;
- the establishment and promotion of fine-chemical manufacturing industries;
- the regulation and control of premises where drugs are manufactured, processed, packed, repacked, stocked or dispensed;
- the amalgamation with, the participation in, or the purchase of undertakings manufacturing, processing or stocking drugs;
- the undertaking of market research on drugs in Sri Lanka or abroad;
- acquisition of trade marks or patents relating to drugs.

The NFC was also expanded, and the chairman of the SPC was made the chairman of a 19-member NFC consisting of three pharmacologists, two consultant physicians, one anaesthetist, two representatives from the Sri Lanka Medical Association (SLMA), two members of the Independent Medical Practitioners Association (IMPA), one representative of the College of Physicians, two representatives of the Ministry of Health, and the Superintendent of the State Medical Stores (SMS). Most of the doctors were members of the pro-drug industry SLMA, while the IMPA was a smaller organisation linked with the socialist wing of the government. The main responsibility of the NFC was to evaluate registration applications for new drugs and to delete obsolete drugs.[8]

Backlash from the drug industry

These actions angered the drug industry, importers, medical representatives and the Sri Lanka Medical Association. A ban on the promotion of drugs led to a reduction in the number of medical representatives, which also meant a sharp reduction in the free samples, gifts and hospitality which members of the medical profession were accustomed to receiving. The drug industry protested loudly, not only because it feared reduced profits but also, and more importantly, because of the possibility of enforced transparency and regulation. Members of the elite who were used to buying costly brands spoke out against the policy while the majority of consumers were confused and remained silent.

The NFC reduced the number of drugs from 2,100 to 600 for the private sector and 500 for the government sector, deleting those which were made up of an 'irrational fixed combination', those 'without clear therapeutic value' and those with high toxicity. A number of imitative, duplicative or 'me-too' drugs were also proscribed by the NFC.

Although drug prices were reduced greatly and no deterioration of health care was evident, the drug companies continued their efforts to undermine the NFC's actions by publishing false reports and propagating rumours through their sales representatives and at the symposia which they organised. Through this barrage of false information they succeeded in convincing many doctors that cheap generic drugs were inferior in quality to their brand-name equivalents. To counter this misinformation, the government could have pointed to the strict quality control measures it employed and to the results of bacteriological tests which showed conclusively that there were no deficiencies in the cheap generic versions. It could also have pointed out that the serious overprescription of antibiotics for minor ailments, which developed resistance to the drugs, was a matter of much greater concern.

Unfortunately, the government took inadequate measures to dispel the medical profession's fears and to produce scientific evidence and reasons for discarding large numbers of brands which had been in use in Sri Lanka for years.

Although most pharmaceuticals imported by the State Pharmaceuticals Corporation (SPC) were from Western market-economy countries (Table 2.3) the drug industry continued its whispering campaign to persuade doctors that all imports were from socialist countries and of poor quality. Most doctors were susceptible to this propaganda. There was no attempt to undertake consumer education through the print and electronic media, so that the public was left in such ignorance that even well-intentioned citizens fell prey to the drug industry's propaganda. Doctors started complaining about interference by the state with their 'clinical freedom and judgement'.

Initially all five TNCs with operations in Sri Lanka, supported by the US Pharmaceutical Manufacturers Association (PMA), refused

Table 2.3: Imports of pharmaceuticals by the State Pharmaceuticals Corporation (SPC) in Sri Lanka

Origin of pharmaceuticals	Percentage of total imports		
	1971	1976	1979*
Western market-economy countries	73.9	60	62
Developing countries	15.7	25.8	29.1
Socialist countries	10.4	14.1	3.9
Others	-	0.1	5.0

*Figures for 1979 were derived through personal communication with SPC.

Source: UNCTAD Secretariat, *Case studies in transfer of technology: Pharmaceutical policies in Sri Lanka*, United Nations, Geneva, June, 1977.

to cooperate and ignored the government regulations. On 10 May 1973, the president of the PMA, Joseph Stetler, wrote a detailed six-page letter of protest to the Sri Lankan Prime Minister. The principal arguments were as follows:

- The prohibitions placed on the industry would inhibit the growth of an indigenous pharmaceutical manufacturing base in Sri Lanka.
- World-wide tender purchasing by the SPC would not guarantee the availability of drugs or raw materials at the time required or at lower prices.
- Companies with high investment in research and development and quality control would be discouraged from bidding.
- The withdrawal of the drug manufacturers' right to select sources of supply was incompatible with their responsibility for quality.
- Inconsistency in the sources of raw material would produce a wide range of medical and therapeutic problems, as well as production sampling and testing difficulties.
- Local companies would no longer receive adequate information concerning new technology and scientific development through the private sector.
- Patent protection was a strong inducement, not only for direct investment, but for the transfer of technology.

Stetler concluded that 'by removing all business incentives and internationally respected property rights', the proposed actions, if implemented, would effectively destroy the modern research-based pharmaceutical industry in Sri Lanka, and that 'the plan would call into question the government's attitude toward any future private investment in the country'.[9] The veiled threat worked, and the government abandoned one aspect of its proposed reforms, namely amendment of the patent law.

Even so, the SPC continued importing patented drugs from non-patent-observing sources. For example, it regularly imported propranolol (whose popular brand name is Inderal) from the Polish company, Polfa, at well under a third of the price charged by the patent holder, ICI. Similarly, Ranbaxy of India supplied diazepam at US$200 per kg, just 3 per cent of the US$7,760 price quoted by the patent holder, Roche, for its brand drug Valium. ICI and Roche threatened to take the SPC to court, but were deterred by an Argentinean Supreme Court ruling in 1970 that a local company which imported a drug patented in the USA from a non-patent-observing country, Italy, 'was acting in the public interest' and not violating patent law.[10]

By December 1973, only Glaxo, a British TNC, had agreed to abide by the government regulations. However, by this time the SPC had conclusively shown that its operation had resulted in savings of up to 93.8 per cent of the costs incurred prior to its establishment (Table 2.4). Confident of success, the government issued stern warnings about penalties for non-compliance. By May 1974, all the transnational companies except Pfizer had begun to comply.

By 1975, the SPC had taken over all importing of raw materials from both transnational and national companies. Most national companies were working in double shifts as their market share was slowly expanding due to the delaying manoeuvres of TNCs who wanted to sabotage the implementation of the policy.

In 1974, when a severe cholera epidemic gripped the country, the SPC asked Pfizer to produce tetracycline capsules with raw materials which it had imported from Hoechst, a West German TNC considerably larger than Pfizer. Pfizer refused to comply with the SPC's request straightaway, using in its defence the statement made by the PMA president in his letter to the Sri Lankan Prime Minister about the problems caused by inconsistency in the sources of raw materials.[11]

The SPC was forced to import tetracycline capsules by air cargo at enormous cost, despite having raw materials at its own warehouses in Colombo. Before any action against Pfizer could be taken, the US ambassador called on the Prime Minister and indicated that the supply of food aid from his country would be in serious jeopardy if any action were taken against Pfizer.[12]

Table 2.4: Comparison of import costs in US$ of intermediate chemicals by the private sector in 1972 and the State Pharmaceuticals Corporation (SPC) in 1973 in Sri Lanka

Intermediate chemicals	Imports by private sector 1972 (Supplier)	(CIF cost per kg in US$)	Imports by SPC in 1973 (Supplier)	(CIF cost per kg in US$)	Savings as percentage of original costs
Tolbutamide	Hoechst	40.62	Hoechst	19.24	52.6
Paracetamol	Sterling	3.24	Polfa	2.52	93.8
Chlorpropamide	Pfizer	126.21	Rhone Poulenc	2.76	14.8
Aspirin	Glaxo	1.16	Pliva	9.46	92.5
Magnesium Hydroxide	Sterling	5.18	Polfa	0.99	14.7
Prednisolone	Organon	632.68	Nichiman	0.61	88.2
Chloramphenicol	Boehringer	25.24	Roussell	321.77	49.1
Cloxacillin	Beecham	606.47	Lepetit	5.46	38.7
Ampicillin	Beecham	569.90	Beecham	135.96	77.6
Tetracycline	Pfizer	98.87	Beecham	95.11	83.3
Chlorpheniramine	Glaxo	411.00	Hoechst	19.72	80.1
			Halewood	52.53	87.3

Source: Lall, Sanjaya, *The Multinational Corporation,* Macmillan, 1980.

The chairman of the SPC was then ordered by the Prime Minister to continue negotiations with Pfizer. Vested interests, both local and foreign, were becoming more successful at slowing down and even halting the pace of reform.

At the end of 1976 the Sri Lanka Communist Party left the coalition government because of disagreement over the handling of general strikes. In February 1977, T. B. Subasinghe, a strong supporter of the SPC, resigned over the government's right-wing policies, especially its submissive behaviour towards TNCs. In March 1977, Professor Bibile also resigned as Chairman of the SPC in protest at the lack of government support for the corporation.

A new government, elected in 1977, transferred the SPC from the Ministry of Industries and Scientific Affairs to the Ministry of Health. Dr Gladys Jayawardena, sister-in-law of the President and a retired microbiologist – and also a critic of the SPC – was appointed the SPC's chairperson. The corporation continued to function, and was responsible for managing the government pharmaceutical production unit and imports for the public sector. However, its former spirit and ideals were lost. The Sri Lankan experience provided a warning to all those who dreamt of an essential drugs policy in Third World countries, about the unholy alliance between US business houses, the US government and local medical establishments. Professor Senaka Bibile, the architect of Sri Lanka's drug policy, died mysteriously on 29 September 1977 while on a field trip in Guyana on behalf of UNCTAD. He was 57 years old.

The introduction of generic names by Pakistan

With the end of army rule in Pakistan on 20 December 1971, Zulfiquar Ali Bhutto, a pro-Western politician backed by nationalists and by China, became President and Chief Martial Law Administrator. The following year, the Bhutto government introduced compulsory generic names for pharmaceuticals.[13]

Transnational companies immediately threatened to withdraw from Pakistan and slowed down their production. Unfortunately, the Pakistan government had no production unit of its own. Nor did the health ministry undertake any programme of public education to inform the people – including doctors – about generic prescription, with the consequence that people were confused by the drug industry's propaganda. Poor-quality drugs also infiltrated the market. In 1976, the generic-drug programme had to be slowed down.[14]

According to Dr Sanjaya Lall, the noted economist and researcher into TNCs and the life of Professor Bibile, Pakistan's generic-drug policy collapsed because insufficient attention was given to factors such as quality control, overcoming the resistance of TNC subsidiaries, persuading doctors of the programme's advantages, and changing the attitudes of elite consumers.[15]

With the change of government in 1978, the programme was finally put into cold storage. Bhutto was hanged in jail on 4 April 1979, under the dictatorship of General Zia ul Haq.

The Hathi Committee in India

The Hathi Committee was set up in 1974 by the Indian Government, in response to a resolution of the Indian Parliament, to investigate the pharmaceutical industry. It consisted of five MPs and eight other members, including civil servants, accountants, social scientists and drug controllers. Its report recommended nationalisation of the drug industry in India, immediate reduction of foreign equity to 40 per cent, and ultimate reduction to 26 per cent. Instead of thousands of brand-name combination drugs, 116 single-ingredient generic drugs were considered adequate, and generic names were to be introduced initially for 13 essential drugs. All new drugs had to be registered and marketed under generic names. In accordance with the spirit of the recommendations made by the Sainsbury and Kefauver committees, the Hathi Committee further recommended that the national formulary be revised and that the Ministry of Health publish a regular medical newsletter with independent medical information on drugs.[16]

However, the sheer power of the pharmaceutical lobby prevented these recommendations from being implemented. TNCs and national manufacturers placed large advertisements in newspapers to discredit the Hathi Committee's recommendations, creating confusion among journalists, doctors and consumers about generics and other aspects of the proposed reforms.[17]

In August 1981, legislation was passed requiring companies to display generic names more prominently than brand names. This attempt at reform was foiled by a high court stay order obtained by German and US transnational companies. In January 1987, just five drugs were made generic: analgin (an irrational combination of aspirin, caffeine and phenacetin produced by the state pharmaceutical unit), aspirin, chlorpromazine, ferrous sulphate and piperazine.

The Indian medical profession at large remained opposed to the generics policy.

Gathering momentum

A number of other initiatives during the 1970s kept the issue of drug policy reform on the international agenda.

Chile   Dr Salvador Allende, a physician and a marxist, was elected President of Chile in 1970 in democratic, Western-style elections. His Government attempted to introduce a national drug policy, covering the procurement, manufacture and promotion of drugs. Around the same time, investigations into Pfizer's activities revealed its involvement in drug smuggling.

Both actions ended with the coup in Chile and the murder of Dr Salvador Allende on 11 September 1973.[18] The involvement of ITT and other transnationals in the overthrow of the Allende Government is well known.

Afghanistan   In 1976, Afghanistan passed its Generic Drug Law with three specific directives:[19]

- Government health institutions were required to use generic drugs only (patented drugs were only to be used when generic equivalents were unavailable).
- Schools of medicine, nursing, pharmacy and veterinary sciences were required to use generic names when teaching about drugs.
- Commercial promotion of patented drugs was prohibited.

The extent of the law was extended in 1979, when all private wholesalers were required to import only those drugs listed in the National Formulary.[20]

Canada   In January 1977, the Canadian Ministry of Health published a Drug Benefit Formulary (DBF) under its Prescriptions At Reasonable Cost Programme. DBF contained approved drug lists with prices under generic names, so that physicians might prescribe the cheapest drugs and patients obtain reimbursement from the government.[21]

USA   In May 1977, the New York State Assembly approved a Generic Drugs Law which required physicians to write generic names in every prescription even if a brand name was specified. This law enabled pharmacists to substitute brand-name drugs with generic-name drugs.[22]

Non-governmental organisations   Throughout the 1970s, health programmes such as Gonoshasthaya Kendra (GK) in rural Bangladesh, the Jamkhed Health Programme in Gujarat, India, and Project Piaxtla in Mexico demonstrated success in primary health care delivery through village-based community health workers and the proper use of selected essential drugs. These experiments were included in the working papers of the Alma Ata Conference convened by WHO in September 1978,[23] which asserted the importance of an integrated primary health care approach within a basic-needs framework.

The Non-Aligned Movement calls for drug regulation

At the Fifth Conference of Heads of State or Government of Non-Aligned Countries, held in Colombo, Sri Lanka, in August 1976, a number of resolutions were adopted in relation to the global drug situation, in particular the need for affordable essential drugs and the need to regulate the fast-growing pharmaceutical industry. The following statements occupied a core position in the declaration issued by the Conference:

'The Conference,

'Recalling the Non-Aligned Action Programme for Economic Cooperation among developing countries adopted at the Conference of Foreign Ministers of Non-Aligned Countries in Georgetown in August 1972 and approved at the Fourth Summit held in Algiers in September 1973,

'Recalling also the economic Declaration of that Summit calling for the further strengthening of economic cooperation among developing countries,

'Noting the inclusion of the production and distribution of medicine and medical substances in the Lima Programme for Mutual Assistance and Solidarity as an additional area of cooperation among developing countries,

'Bearing in mind the possibilities for joint action by developing countries, identified in the study commissioned by UNCTAD [the United Nations Conference on Trade and Development] on major issues in the transfer of technology to the developing countries in the pharmaceutical industry,

'1. Endorses the recommendations of the Group of Experts on Pharmaceuticals which met in Georgetown in July 1976 and which proposes among other things:
'(a) the preparation of a list of priority pharmaceutical needs of each developing country and the formulation of a basic model list of such needs as a general guideline for action by the developing countries;
'(b) the establishment of a national buying agency to undertake the purchase and supply of pharmaceuticals;
'(c) that in the context of the revision of the industrial property systems, consideration be given to excluding pharmaceutical products from

the grant of patent rights or alternatively the curtailment of the duration of patents for pharmaceuticals;

'(d) the elimination, wherever possible, of brand names and the adoption of the generic names for pharmaceuticals; and provision of information only from official sources;

'(e) the establishment by each developing country of its own pharmaceutical industry as appropriate, beginning with formulation and packaging and building up to more complex activities;

'(f) the creation of regional Cooperative Pharmaceutical Production and Technology Centres (COPPTECS), as proposed by UNCTAD and UNIDO [the United Nations Industrial Development Organization], in order to draw up drug lists, to coordinate research and development, facilitate the transfer of technology, collect and disseminate information on pharmaceutical uses and prices and on the technological capabilities among member countries and also to coordinate the production and exchange of drugs between member countries as well as different regional centres;

'2. Invites the relevant international organisations such as UNCTAD, UNIDO, WHO and UNDP [United Nations Development Programme] to assist in the achievements of the objectives outlined in operative paragraph 1 above with particular regard to the establishment of appropriate National Pharmaceutical Centres in developing countries and Regional Cooperative Pharmaceutical Production and Technology Centres (COPPTECS) among them.

'3. Decides further that the coordinator of the trade, transport and industry sector of the Non-Aligned Action Programme for Economic Cooperation among developing countries should take the necessary follow-up action to ensure early implementation of the provisions of this resolution.'[24]

WHO's bombshell

Under the leadership of Dr Halfdan Mahler, appointed Director-General in May 1973 (and re-elected in 1978 and 1983), WHO saw two qualitative changes in its agenda. It was influenced by Dr Mahler's concern about the non-availability of technological gains, especially in the form of essential drugs, to the vast majority of the people who needed them most, and about the curative bias in health care systems.

In 1974, Mahler began promoting the concept of basic health services, especially for rural and peri-urban areas, leading to the Alma Ata Declaration in 1978. In 1975, he began outlining possible new policies for making quality essential drugs widely available at reasonable cost.[25] In December 1976 he convened an informal consultation on a model essential drugs list with five representatives of the International Federation of Pharmaceutical Manufacturers' Associations (IFPMA), including its president.[26]

In 1977, a year after the Non-Aligned Movement's resolution, WHO appointed an Expert Committee on the Selection of Essential Drugs. This met between 17 and 21 October and was chaired by Professor D. L. Azarnoff, Professor of Medicine and Pharmacology at the Kansas University Medical Center, USA, and a distinguished and respected academic. The committee had a total of eight members, of whom five were from Third World countries.

The Expert Committee's report, *The Selection of Essential Drugs*, which was just 36 pages in length, was to have far-reaching implications and is arguably one of the most important documents ever published by WHO.[27] It asserted that drugs are important, but alone are not sufficient to ensure adequate health, and that 'for the treatment of certain conditions, non-pharmacological forms of therapy, or no therapy at all, may be preferable'. The document stated that the demand for drugs was made 'greater than actual needs' through the promotional activities of drug manufacturers. It argued that drug lists should be restricted to those products which have been proven to be 'therapeutically effective' and of 'acceptable safety'. 'Essential drugs' were those that were 'indispensable ... for the health needs of the population' and also available at a reasonable cost, since cost constraints were a major consideration in both Third World and industrialised countries. The guidelines for selection of essential drugs were to be understood as a tentative identification of a 'common core' of basic needs which had 'universal relevance and applicability'. Reviewing of drugs lists should take place 'at least once a year and whenever necessary', and new drugs should be introduced only if they offered 'distinct advantages over drugs previously selected'.[28]

The Expert Committee emphasised the importance of educating both prescribers and consumers. It stated that education of health care professionals about drugs 'should begin early in their training and be continued not only throughout their formal training period but throughout their entire professional life', and that to minimise bias about drug information 'it will probably be necessary for these educational efforts to be supported by the government'. Further-more, both prescriber and consumer 'must be persuaded that when therapeutically equivalent, the cheaper generic products are as effective as the more expensive proprietary name products'. Finally, the Expert Committee urged WHO to disseminate the report widely, reiterating that 'health care can be considerably improved in terms of both effectiveness and economy through the selection of essential drugs'.[29]

The little book was a bombshell for the drug industry. It was bitterly criticised by the US Pharmaceutical Manufacturers Association (PMA) which stated on 10 April 1978: '[The] medical and economic arguments presented by WHO as justification for an essential drugs list are fallacious and ... adoption of this recommendation could result in suboptimal medical care and might reduce health standards already attained'.[30] True to form, it argued that an essential drugs list would discourage the pharmaceutical industry from investing in research.

The IFPMA council passed a resolution stating that it had 'serious reservations about the policies recommended' and was 'deeply concerned' by the manner in which these policies were being 'represented and promoted by the World Health Organization'.[31] To strengthen its lobbying with UN agencies, and specifically with WHO, in 1978 the IFPMA appointed Michael Peretz, a man well versed in WHOs drug policies, as its first full-time executive vice-president.

The IFPMA resolution had its desired effect. Although Professor Azarnoff had been drawn into the industry as full-time Senior Vice-President of the US transnational G.D. Searle & Co, he remained a member of the Expert Committee on the Selection of Essential Drugs. The impact of the resolution and of Professor Azarnoff's presence on the committee became evident in the next edition of *The Selection of Essential Drugs* (published in 1979), which, although increased in length from 36 to 44 pages, was reduced in content and impact.[32] The second edition made it crystal clear that essential drugs were for Third World countries only and made no reference to the universal relevance and applicability of a model list, cost considerations, the effect of cost in affluent nations on the education of health professionals and consumers about generic drugs, the implication of the promotional activities of the manufacturers and the importance of limited drugs lists and formularies. Furthermore, the Expert Committee no longer called on WHO to 'widely disseminate' the book to member states but stressed the 'importance of an exchange of information with the pharmaceutical industry on drugs'.[33]

Although officially recommended by the World Health Assembly in 1978, an Action Programme on Essential Drugs (APED) was not instituted by WHO until 1981. A resolution at the 35th World Health

Assembly in April 1982 urged member states to adopt essential drugs lists, generic names, tougher drug legislation, strategies for reduction of drug prices and a code of drug marketing practice.[34] Nevertheless, WHO has not always accorded APED the status it requires.

Notes

1. Keayla, B. K., *Patents Regime: Indian Experience and Options Available*, National Working Group on Patent Laws, New Delhi, 1992.
2. Department of Justice, Restrictive Trade Practices Commission (RTPC), *Report Concerning Manufacture, Distribution and Sale of Drugs*, Ottawa, 1963.
3. Banks Committee, *Report of the Committee to Examine Patent System and Patent Law*, HMSO, London, 1970.
4. Rangarao B. V., 'Foreign Technology in the Indian Pharmaceutical Industry', paper presented at the International Seminar on Technology Transfer, New Delhi, 11–13 December 1972.
5. Bibile, S. (ed), *Ceylon Hospitals Formulary*, Ceylon Government Press, Colombo, 1959.
6. Bibile, S. and Wickremasinghe, S. A., The *Management of Pharmaceuticals in Ceylon*, Industrial Board of Ceylon, Colombo, 1971.
7. *Government Gazette Extraordinary*, No. 14976, Ceylon Government Press, Colombo, 22 September 1971, quoted in Bibile, S./UNCTAD, *Case Studies in Transfer of Technology: Pharmaceutical Policies in Sri Lanka*, UNCTAD Secretariat, United Nations, Geneva, June 1977.
8. Bibile, S./UNCTAD, *Case Studies in Transfer of Technology: Pharmaceutical Policies in Sri Lanka*, UNCTAD Secretariat, United Nations, Geneva, June 1977.
9. Stetler, J. C., President, PMA, letter to the Honourable Mrs Sirimavo R. D. Banderanaike, Prime Minister, Ceylon, 10 May 1973.
10. Ledogar, R. J., 'Hungry for profits: The US Food and Drug multinationals in Latin America', IDOC, New York, 1975, quoted in Lall, S. and Bibile, S., 'The Political Economy of Controlling Transnationals: The Pharmaceutical Industry in Sri Lanka, 1972–76', *Economic and Political Weekly*, Bombay, special issue, August 1977.
11. Stetler, J. C., op. cit.
12. Muller, M., *The Health of Nations: A North–South Investigation*, Faber and Faber, London, 1982.
13. Government of Guyana in collaboration with UNCTAD/UNDTCD/UNIDO/WHO, *Pharmaceuticals in the Developing World: Policies on Drugs, Trade and Production*, Vol. 1, General Report, 'Economic and Technical Cooperation Among Developing Countries in the Pharmaceutical Sector', June 1979; and Saeed, Hilda, 'Other Experiences: Pakistan', in *Prescription for Change*, Philippine Center for Investigative Journalism/Dag Hammarskjöld Foundation, Sweden, 1992.
14. Saeed, Hilda, op. cit.
15. Lall, S. and Bibile, S., 'The Political Economy of Controlling Transnationals: The Pharmaceutical Industry in Sri Lanka, 1972–76', *Economic and Political Weekly*, Bombay, special issue, August 1977.
16. Hathi Committee, *Report of the Committee on the Drugs and Pharmaceutical Industry*, Ministry of Petroleum and Chemicals, Government of India, New Delhi, April 1975.

17. One advertisement which read 'Would you rather have your doctor choose a medicine for you—or somebody else?' appeared in *Indian Express*, 29 December 1980, and *India Today*, 1–15 February 1981, and subsequently in many other national and regional newspapers.

18. Heller, T., *Poor Health, Rich Profits: Multinational Drug Companies in the Third World*, Spokesman Books, London, 1977.

19. Generic Drugs Law, Resolution 418 of 1976, Republic of Afganistan, quoted in *Case Studies in Transfer of Technology: Pharmaceutical Policies in Sri Lanka*, op. cit.

20. Government of Guyana, op. cit.

21. *Drug Benefit Formulary*, Ministry of Health, Ontario, January 1977.

22. Bibile, S./UNCTAD, *Case Studies in Transfer of Technology: Pharmaceutical Policies in Sri Lanka*, op. cit.

23. Djuknavic, V. and Mach, E. P., *Alternative Approaches to Basic Health Needs in Developing Countries*, a joint UNICEF/WHO study, WHO, Geneva, 1975.

24. 'Resolution on co-operation among developing countries in the production, procurement and distribution of pharmaceuticals', Fifth Conference of Heads of State or Government of Non-Aligned Countries, Colombo, Sri Lanka, 1976, A/31/197 (Annex IV: Political and economic resolutions, NAC/CONF.5/S/RES.25).

25. WHO, Official Records No. 226, Annexure 13 of WHA 28.66, World Health Organization, Geneva, 1975.

26. Kanji, N., Hardon, A., Hammeijer, J. W., Mamdani, M. and Walt, G., *Drugs Policy in Developing Countries*, Zed Books, 1992.

27. WHO, *The Selection of Essential Drugs*, Report of a WHO Expert Committee, Technical Report Series 615, World Health Organization, Geneva, 1977.

28. Ibid.

29. Ibid.

30. PMA, *The Pharmaceutical Industry: International Issues and Answers*, Pharmaceutical Manufacturers Association, Washington DC, April 1979.

31. Quoted in PMA, 'Issue: The selection of essential drugs', in *The Pharmaceutical Industry: International Issues and Answers*, Pharmaceutical Manufacturers Association, Washington DC, April 1979.

32. WHO, *The Selection of Essential Drugs*, Second report of the WHO Expert Committee, TRS641, World Health Organization, Geneva, 1979.

33. Ibid.

34. WHO, Action Programme on Essential Drugs, Report by the Executive Board Ad-hoc Committee on Drug Policies on behalf of the Executive Board, 35th World Health Assembly (A 35/7), 1 April 1982, and Annexure 1, Relevant Health Assembly Resolutions WHA 31/32.

3

Bangladesh National Drug Policy 1982

On 14 August 1947, Britain left an independent but divided Indian subcontinent. The provinces with a Muslim majority and those with a Hindu majority became, respectively, Pakistan and India. The province of East Pakistan was separated from the rest of Pakistan by 1,100 miles of Indian territory.

In 1971, the geo-political face of the subcontinent changed once again. In March 1971, when East Pakistan began its struggle for independence, it was supported and aided by India. China remained silent, and the USA sent the 7th US Fleet to the Bay of Bengal in support of Pakistan but did not actually participate in the war. With the help of India, Bangladesh emerged as an independent country on 16 December 1971 and adopted a non-aligned socialist position. It attended the summits of the Non-Aligned Movement (NAM) in 1973 and 1976 and endorsed all the resolutions made on both occasions.

The NAM declaration on drug regulation in August 1976 (see chapter 2) provided a legitimate political context for the introduction of drug legislation. News about reform attempts elsewhere had created considerable interest in Bangladesh: in particular, the experience of India, Pakistan and Sri Lanka provided insight into the difficulties of drug regulation as well as creating a greater determination to prepare well and to persevere.

1971–81: Political events and the struggle for health

A series of steps was taken in Bangladesh throughout the 1970s, leading up to the enactment of a radical and far-reaching National Drug Policy (NDP) in 1982. The new commitment to action on

45

health was attributable to the historical convergence of a number of important factors and forces.

The members of the first Planning Commission, as well as most of the civil servants in the post-independence government, had participated in the independence struggle and were committed to building an egalitarian Bangladesh. Besides the official effort, many professionals who had been freedom fighters returned to embark on independent development efforts. These activists were concerned to ensure that the rural majority were given access to health care and other services, and they also started to communicate scientific subjects in the language of the people. The most popular Bengali weekly, *Bichitra*, started publishing articles about the drug companies, their unethical practices and the flooding of Third World markets with inappropriate and harmful drugs, many of which had long before been withdrawn in industrialised countries. One *Bichitra* cover story in 1976, entitled 'Drug imperialism' and full of revelations about Roche, the Sainsbury Committee's report and the British Monopolies Commission, caused a great stir among civil servants, politicians and the general public.

The experience of the freedom struggle had created both an aspiration for better conditions and an awareness among politicians and bureaucrats of the problems of health care, especially concerning the affordability and availability of essential drugs.

Health in Bangladesh in the 1970s

The problems facing the country were summarised in the First Five Year Plan document of 1973: 'Bangladesh inherited a poor, undiversified economy, characterised by an underdeveloped infrastructure, stagnant agriculture, and rapidly growing population. She had suffered from years of colonial exploitation and missed opportunities, with debilitating effects on initiative and enterprise.'[1]

It was estimated in 1972 that Bangladesh had a population of 74 million people, a crude birth rate of 47 per 1,000 people, a crude death rate of 17 per 1,000 and an infant mortality rate of 140 per 1,000 live births. Maternal mortality was estimated to be 30 per 1,000 pregnancies. The high death rate of 260 per 1,000 children under five years of age was mostly due to preventable disease and malnutrition.

This dismal state of affairs was largely attributable to inadequate and badly distributed health facilities. Essential drugs were highly priced and not easily available. The Planning Commission observed:

'Many so-called manufacturers are engaged in bottling drugs imported in bulk, acting indirectly as the sales agents of foreign firms. Quality control of drugs is insufficient and spurious drugs are quite common'.[2]

Twenty years later, the situation of Bangladesh and other neighbouring countries showed little improvement (Table 3.1).

The socialist aspirations which characterised the independence struggle of Bangladesh were reflected in its First Five Year Plan. The Plan document specifically stated as part of its health sector objectives:

- the creation of a health infrastructure in the rural areas to provide integrated and comprehensive health and family planning services;
- improved availability of life-saving drugs and immunisation;
- an adequate supply of essential drugs through the development of domestic manufacture, and imports on the basis of actual requirements;
- decentralisation of the drug supply system through the creation of depots and sub-depots in the country;
- the review and amendment of the Drug Licensing and Drug Control Acts.[3]

Because of its commitment to reform, Bangladesh did not become a signatory to the Paris Convention on Patents in 1973 which essentially protects the interests of industrialised countries.

One element of the government's health care programme was centralised procurement of cheaper generic drugs, often through barter arrangements with European socialist countries. This was as much for economic as for political reasons, since there was a shortage of foreign exchange for buying goods from the West. Bulk purchases were regularly made through the state-run Trading Corporation of Bangladesh (TCB) which, unlike Sri Lanka's State Pharmaceuticals Corporation, imported pharmaceuticals as well as other commodities and distributed them to both the public and private sectors.

Predictably, transnational corporations were hostile to this approach. Seeing imports from Eastern European countries rising every year, and in an attempt to force the Government to spend its meagre resources on importing drugs from western industrialised countries, they embarked on a campaign of misinformation among the medical profession and elite consumers, as had happened in Sri Lanka.[4]

Table 3.1: Selected human development indicators in South Asian countries

Country	Population (in million)	GNP (US$ per capita)	Adult literacy (percentage of population aged 15+)	Access to safe water (percentage of population)	Infant mortality rate (per 1,000 live births)	Under-five mortality rate (per 1,000 live births)	Maternal mortality rate (per 100,000 live births)	Life expectancy at birth
Bangladesh	119.5	220	37	-	109	150	650	52
Bhutan	1.6	190	41	31	131	200	800	48
India	880.1	330	50	-	89	130	550	60
Nepal	20.6	180	27	42	100	155	850	53
Pakistan	124.9	400	36	56	99	130	600	58
Sri Lanka	17.7	500	89	71	24	30	180	71

Source: Human Development Report 1994, UNDP, New York, 1994.

Joining hands with importers of foreign drugs, they began to spread rumours about the dubious quality of drugs from Eastern Europe and the political motivation for increasing imports from socialist countries. In response, Sheikh Mujibur Rahman, the Prime Minister and leader of the ruling party, the Awami League, ordered a Commission of Enquiry which failed to prove any political motive. Allegations of inferior quality could not be substantiated either. Even then the campaign by TNCs continued.

The US Government was likewise seriously displeased that Bangladesh continued to trade with socialist countries, including Cuba. This led ultimately to the withholding of wheat exports from the USA during the 1974 famine in Bangladesh when several hundred thousand people died.[5]

As the Government's support for socialism and austerity declined, the TCB's share of imports dropped from 40 per cent to 10 per cent by 1974. As a result, drug prices started shooting up.

Sheikh Mujibur Rahman was assassinated on 15 August 1975. General Ziaur Rahman, a freedom fighter, took power as the country's new leader on 7 November 1975. The new government began work to amend legislation of drugs. The existing Drug Act of 1940 was grossly inadequate for the control of prices of pharmaceutical raw materials and processed drugs; it also largely failed to prevent the appearance of substandard and spurious drugs on the market, unethical promotion, and the proliferation of harmful and useless drugs.

In 1979, the Bangladesh Ansudh Shilpa Shamity (BASS – the Bangladesh Association of Pharmaceutical Industries), comprised mainly of transnational and a few large national pharmaceutical companies and trading houses, discovered that the then Minister of Health, Dr M. M. Huq, a retired colonel and a trustee of Gonoshasthaya Kendra (People's Health Centre), had finalised the drafting of rational and tougher drug legislation. They not only blocked the introduction of the bill but were also successful in removing Dr Huq from his ministerial post. This action was achieved through the collusion of the Minister of Industry, who also held the post of Deputy Prime Minister. He was a chartered accountant whose firm acted for a majority of TNCs in Bangladesh.

Fortunately, before leaving his post, Dr Huq had agreed to the establishment of Gonoshasthaya Pharmaceutical Ltd (GPL) to produce and market high-quality essential drugs at reasonable prices. Gonoshasthaya Kendra had struggled for four years for authorisation from the ministry to set up this pharmaceutical factory. Later on,

GPL played an important role in the formulation of the Bangladesh National Drug Policy (NDP) and in stabilising cheaper drug prices in Bangladesh by providing information to the government on the economics of drug production and international prices of raw materials.

President Ziaur Rahman was killed on 29 May 1981, and Justice M. A. Sattar, an old man of 82, became President. Justice Sattar was replaced by General Hussain Muhammad Ershad in a bloodless military coup on 24 March 1982.

The formation of the Expert Committee

Only a month later, on 27 April 1982, the Military Government appointed an eight-member Expert Committee to review the drug situation in the country and make recommendations for a National Drug Policy consistent with the health needs of the country.[6]

The members of the Expert Committee were:

- Professor Nurul Islam (Chairman), Professor of Medicine, Director of the Institute of Postgraduate Medicine and Research (IPGMR) and Dean of Postgraduate Medicine at Dhaka University;
- Dr Humayun K. M. A. Hye, Director of Medical Education and Hospitals, a pharmacologist and formerly Director of the Drug Administration;
- Professor M. A. Mannan, a pharmacologist who later became the Vice-Chancellor of Dhaka University;
- Professor Mobarak Ali, Director of the Institute of Ophthalmology, Dhaka;
- Professor M. Q. K. Talukdar, Associate Professor of Paediatrics, IPGMR;
- Dr Azizur Rahman, Surgeon and President of the Bangladesh Private Medical Practitioners Association, Dhaka;
- Dr Zafrullah Chowdhury, Surgeon, health activist and Projects Co-ordinator of Gonoshasthaya Kendra, Savar, Dhaka;
- Dr Nurul Anwar (Member Secretary), pharmacologist, pharmaceutical chemist and Director of the Drug Administration.

The committee consisted of three categories of people: academics, regulatory personnel and health activists. Three of the committee members were former freedom fighters in the liberation struggle against Pakistan. The health minister, Major General M. Shamsul

Huq, had also participated in the freedom struggle and was himself a doctor.

It was a shrewd move on the part of the government to include Professor Nurul Islam, and to make him Chairman of the committee, as he was closely linked with the main opposition party, the Awami League, led by Ms Sheikh Hasina Wazed, daughter of the late president.

The committee had a number of significant characteristics. First, no representative of the transnational drug industry was included, for obvious reasons. This principle led to the exclusion of the chief executives of the Bangladesh Medical Association (BMA) because of formal associations with transnationals. However, all six members of the Expert Committee were general members of the BMA. Moreover, Dr Humayun Hye was one of the two members of the BMA's Drug Evaluation Sub-Committee. The subcommittee's other member, Dr Ahmad Rafiq, was the general manager of Albert David, a nationalised drug company. He was also a writer and had been closely associated with the freedom fighters during the siege of Dhaka in 1971. Although not an official member of the Expert Committee, Dr Rafiq was frequently consulted in confidence and provided a wealth of inside information on the drug industry in Bangladesh.

Second, it was a well-informed committee. Many of its members had been profoundly influenced by a number of books published in the 1970s which exposed the misdeeds of the drug companies and promoted new policies on drugs. Among these were: *Who Needs the Drug Companies,*[7] *Pills, Profits and Politics,*[8] *The Drugging of the Americas,*[9] *The Selection of Essential Drugs,*[10] *Insult or Injury,*[11] and *Pills That Do Not Work.*[12] Having access to the information revealed in these publications was, for the committee, a crucial factor affecting the drafting of the NDP. Some members were also well acquainted with the problems experienced by India, Pakistan and Sri Lanka in their attempts to regulate drugs and were aware of the efforts under way in Europe and the USA to bring about changes in the pharmaceutical industry through the democratic process. They were able privately to bring these matters to the attention of the Minister of Health.

Third, this was probably the first and last drug committee in Bangladesh which did not include a civil servant. At the time that the Expert Committee was set up, the health secretary, M. Siddiqur Rahman, was in Geneva, attending the 35th World Health Assembly. If he had been in Bangladesh, he would no doubt have appointed some bureaucrats as committee members. Third World countries, whether under democratic or military rule, are usually governed by the civil bureaucrats alone, or by a combination of the civil service and the military bureaucracy. Ministers, appointed politically or otherwise, are usually figureheads.

The work of the Expert Committee

At its first meeting, on 28 April 1982, the Expert Committee made a rough calculation that most practitioners, whether general practitioners or specialists, usually prescribe from a total of around 50 drugs and that the figure rarely exceeds 100. On the basis of this, it decided that a drugs list in line with the advice given in WHO's *The Selection of Essential Drugs* should be drawn up.[13]

Unfortunately, only the previous (1977) edition of this publication was available in the library of the Institute of Postgraduate Medicine and Research. The chairman of the committee immediately phoned WHO's country representative in Dhaka for a copy of the latest (1979) edition. The WHO representative did not have the current edition either but promised to acquire eight copies from WHO's regional office in New Delhi. These were delivered to the chairman of the committee on 10 May 1982.[14] In the meantime, since one member had his own copy of the latest edition of the publication, the committee was able to refer to this.

Three other important decisions were taken on the first day. First, it was decided that current, authentic and unbiased scientific literature would be used extensively, and various specialists would be consulted and asked for their opinion on the basis of 'scientific reasoning'. Deletion of a drug would be recommended following a unanimous decision by the committee. Second, it was decided that the report, including rationale and plan of action, should be short enough for decision-makers to read in one sitting; it was to be written in simple language, avoiding all jargon and difficult scientific words, for easy understanding by all concerned persons. Third, to prevent the leakage of information, the committee would not use any secretarial staff from the Drug Administration. All members vowed strict secrecy until the document could be made public by the government. Meetings were held behind closed doors and no information filtered out, a state of affairs which angered the pharmaceutical industry. *The Pulse*, a weekly journal financed by the industry, criticised the committee for not consulting the industry and for holding meetings behind an 'iron curtain'.[15]

The committee's view was that the ideal drug is a single-ingredient product and that unnecessary combinations not only increase cost and proliferate the number of products but also give rise to side effects and adverse reactions because of the instability of the compound or its limited life span. Members of the committee reached a unanimous decision that 16 criteria should guide the evaluation of all registered/licensed pharmaceutical products already manufactured in, or imported into, Bangladesh as well as the evaluation of all new drugs for which licences and registration were sought (see pp. 54–55).

These criteria covered: the introduction and reformulation of single-ingredient products, especially antibiotics and analgesics; strict restriction of combination drugs, limiting the exceptions to a very few products; elimination of placebo products and drugs without adequate scientific and medical grounds to justify their existence; and, last but not least, a ban on toll manufacture. Moreover, domestic companies were given the exclusive right to manufacture antacids and oral vitamins.

Syrups and liquid forms of medicines for adults were discouraged in consideration of the economy of the country and the purchasing power of the people. In general, liquid forms have no added advantage but are more expensive because of the extra cost of bottle, cap, sugar, flavours and excipients.

The first 11 criteria were based exclusively on scientific reasoning while number 14 was based on political and economic considerations as well: the hope was that TNCs, no longer allowed to manufacture or market antacids and oral vitamins, would concentrate on producing more useful drugs such as antibiotics and other life-saving drugs, and that the ban would also help in preventing monopoly cartels. The remaining four criteria (12, 13, 15 and 16) were for the benefit of the local national industry.

The impact: all companies affected

At the time that the National Drug Policy (NDP) was formulated there were 177 licensed pharmaceutical manufacturers in the country, of which eleven small national companies were no longer producing. Out of the remaining 166 companies, seven small national pharmaceutical factories had had their licence suspended owing to irregularities. The British TNC Reckitt & Colman had no factory of its own, but produced only one brand product, Dispirin (aspirin), on a toll basis in a very small national factory. SmithKline and French

The 16 criteria

1. The combination of an antibiotic with another antibiotic, or antibiotics with corticosteroid, or other active substances will be prohibited.

The manufacture in liquid form of antibiotics harmful to children (e.g. tetracycline) will not be allowed.

2. The combination of analgesics in any form is not allowed as there is no therapeutic advantage and it only increases toxicity, especially in the case of kidney damage. The combination of analgesics with iron, vitamins or alcohol is not allowed.

3. The use of codeine in any combination form is not allowed as it causes addiction.

4. In general, no combination drugs will be used unless there is absolutely no alternative single drug available for treatment or if no alternative single drug is cost-effective for the purpose.

Certain exceptions will be made in the cases of eye, skin, respiratory and haemorrhoidal preparations, co-trimaxazole, oral rehydration salts, antimalarial, iron-folic, etc., as well as certain vitamin preparations, allowing combinations of more than one active ingredient in one product.

5. Vitamins should be prepared as single ingredient products with the exception of B complex. Members of vitamin B complex, with the exception of B12, may be combined into one product. B12 should always be produced as a single-ingredient injectable product. Other members of B complex may also be produced as a single-ingredient product (e.g. B1, B2, B6, etc). The combining of Vitamins with any other ingredient such as minerals, glycerophosphate, etc., will not be allowed. Vitamins may be produced in tablet, capsule and injectable form only.

No liquid forms will be permitted because of wastage of financial resources and the tremendous misuse involved. However, the manufacture of paediatric liquid multivitamins (with no B12, E, K and/or minerals) will be allowed in bottles of 15 ml size with droppers. The manufacture of paediatric liquid preparations of single ingredient vitamins will also be allowed in bottles of up to 15 ml with droppers.

6. No cough mixtures, throat lozenges, gripe water, alkalis, etc. should be manufactured or imported as these are of little or no therapeutic value and amount to great wastage of our meagre resources.

7. The sale of tonics, enzyme mixtures/preparations and so-called restorative products flourish on consumer ignorance. Most are habit-forming and, with the exception of pancreatin and lactase, these are of

no therapeutic value. Henceforth, local manufacture or importation of such products will be discontinued. However, pancreatin and lactase may be manufactured and/or imported as single-ingredient products.

8.   Some drugs are being manufactured with only a slight difference in composition from another product but having similar action. This confuses both patients and doctors. This will not be allowed.

9.   Products of doubtful, little or no therapeutic value, and rather sometimes harmful and subject to misuse, will be banned.

10. All prescription chemicals and galenical preparations not included in the latest edition of the *British Pharmacopeia* or the *British Pharmaceutical Codex* will be prohibited.

11. Certain drugs, in spite of known serious side-effects and the possibility of misuse, may be produced in limited quantity for restricted use if the risk:benefit ratio is favourable. These will be prescribed by specialists only.

12. The importing of a drug which is the same as one produced in the country, or a close substitute for it, may not be imported, as a measure of protection for the local industry. However, if local production is far short of need, this condition may be relaxed in some cases.

13. A basic pharmaceutical raw material which is locally manufactured will be given protection by disallowing it or its substitute to be imported if sufficient quantity is available in the country.

14. The role of multinationals in providing medicine for this country is acknowledged with appreciation. In view of the calibre of machinery and technical know-how which lies in their hands for producing important and innovative drugs for the country, the task of producing antacids and vitamins will lie solely with the national companies, leaving the multinationals free to concentrate their efforts and resources on those items not so easily produced by smaller national companies. Multinationals will, however, be allowed to produce injectable vitamins as single-ingredient products.

15. No foreign brands may be manufactured under license in any factory in Bangladesh if the same or similar products are available/ manufactured in Bangladesh, as this leads to unnecessarily high prices and payment of royalties. In the light of this policy, all existing licensing agreements should be reviewed.

16. No multinational company without their own factory in Bangladesh will be allowed to market their products after manufacturing them in another factory in Bangladesh on a toll basis.

Table 3.2:   Number of foreign companies exporting drugs to Bangladesh in 1981–82 by country of origin

Country of origin	Number of companies	Country of origin	Number of of companies
UK	29	Denmark	3
USA	12	Greece	3
India	11	Holland	3
Switzerland	10	Hong Kong	3
Germany	9	China	2
Japan	7	France	2
Hungary	6	Bulgaria	1
Italy	6	Ireland	1
Belgium	4	Philippines	1
Yugoslavia	4	Poland	1
Australia	3	Singapore	1
		Total:	122

had just spent Taka 2.8 million on establishing a factory in a rented house in Dhaka and had started production in April 1982. In all, there were 122 foreign companies exporting drugs to Bangladesh from 23 countries (Table 3.2). The total number of registered products, both locally produced and imported, was 4,340.

All registered products manufactured locally by both national and transnational companies were examined. Registered imported products, irrespective of the country of origin, were evaluated on the same basis.

In all, 1,742 drugs were found to be harmful, inappropriately formulated or therapeutically ineffective. Out of this total, 176 were produced locally by TNCs, 617 were imported and 949 were manufactured by 156 local manufacturers.

Measured against the 16 criteria for evaluation, TNCs had marketed more irrational antibiotic combination drugs than local national companies had done (Table 3.3). Criteria 13–16 were not applied to imported drugs but to 22 drugs produced locally by TNCs, while criterion 12 was applied to 248 imported drugs only. Measured against criteria 5, 6, 7, and 9, 1,089 drugs were found undesirable. Capitalist countries had exported more ineffective, useless or harmful drugs than socialist countries. Among the offenders, West German and Swiss companies ranked very high.

Table 3.3: Numbers of drugs banned in the Drugs (Control) Ordinance, 1982, of Bangladesh according to criterion and by country of origin

Criterion	Locally produced drugs		Imported drugs								
	National company	TNC	USA	UK	Germany	Switzerland	Hungary	India*	Japan	Others
1	19	45	14	14	4	2	1	1	2	28
2	54	10	1	11	2	6	2	-	1	2
3	2	-	-	-	1	2	2	-	-	-
4	5	1	-	2	4	2	2	2	-	-
5	149	37	11	10	20	10	4	-	2	25
6	262	13	2	8	-	-	-	-	-	4
7	181	8	2	8	2	1	-	-	1	-
8	18	11	-	-	-	-	-	-	-	-
9	192	25	15	30	20	16	6	6	8	14
10	39	1	2	6	1	2	-	-	-	1
11	3**	3**	1	3	24	3	3	1	1	5
12	-	-	16	45	-	29	15	10	-	109
13	1	3	-	-	-	-	-	-	-	-
14	-	10	-	-	-	-	-	-	-	-
15	24	9***	-	-	-	-	-	-	-	-
16	7		-	-	-	-	-	-	-	-
Total number of drugs	949	176	64	137	79	82	35	20	15	185
Number of companies	156	10	12	29	9	10	6	11	7	38

* Among 11 exporting companies, 6 were India-based TNC subsidiaries and 5 were Indian companies. ** Later placed on the Restricted List. *** Reckett and Coleman, the only producer of soluble aspirin, was exempted.

The banned drugs concerned were placed in one of three categories:

- **Schedule I:** The committee recommended immediate stoppage of production of drugs listed in Schedule I. These drugs were to be collected from pharmacies and destroyed within three months of the acceptance of the report.
- **Schedule II:** Drugs in this category were to be reformulated within six months on the basis of the guidelines suggested by the committee.
- **Schedule III:** A maximum of nine months was allowed for utilisation of Schedule III drugs.

Importation of raw materials for Schedule I and II drugs was prohibited.

Each of the 166 manufacturing companies in the country except Reckitt & Colman was affected by the recommendations of the Expert Committee. Reckitt & Colman was exempted on special consideration as the company was the sole manufacturer of soluble aspirin: the product was also manufactured in a small local factory on a toll basis. Reckitt & Coleman had no other product. Local companies were the worst affected. G-sulphathalazole, one of the products of Gonoshasthaya Pharmaceutical Ltd (GPL), was included in Schedule III.

A total of 1,742 inessential or ineffective drugs out of 4,340 products may sound like a high proportion. However, Senake Bibile had reported in 1977 in Sri Lanka: 'Vitamin preparations, soluble aspirin and cough remedies account for over 50 per cent of the total products. They are elegantly presented and heavily promoted.' He had also pointed out that the two largest firms in Sri Lanka made 18 different combinations of vitamins and that these were taken by the well-nourished, who did not need them.[16] An UNCTAD study in Nepal in 1980 found that out of 2,000 products in the drug market, 733 – or more than a third – were tonics. Although anaemia and malnutrition were major health problems amongst the poor, they were unable to buy these expensive, non-essential combination products.[17]

Twenty-two out of 56 drug products marketed by Glaxo (Bangladesh) in 1981–82 were vitamins and tonics. Only three of these were marketed in Britain, of which two were basic preparations of vitamin A and vitamin B complex.

Major recommendations

The National Drug Policy (NDP) document was short, and written in simple language. The guidelines for evaluation of existing drugs took up nine pages, and the essential drugs lists and evaluation of brands another 70 pages. The objective of the NDP was to ensure that procurement, local production, quality control, distribution and utilisation of all drugs came under unified legislative and administrative control. The NDP was to be the uniform policy for both the private and the public sector, and for both the traditional and the modern medical systems. It was intended to be an integral part of a national health policy.

The major recommendations were as follows:

a) There should be a basic list of 150 essential drugs and a supplementary list of 100 specialised drugs to be prescribed by specialists and consultants. The basic list was subdivided as follows:

Level I: for use by village health workers – 12 drugs
Level II: for use in primary health care up to Thana Health Complex (THC) level – 45 drugs (inclusive of drugs for Level I)
Level III: for use up to tertiary level – 150 drugs (inclusive of drugs for Levels I & II)

Interestingly, the committee could name only 76 specialised drugs in the supplementary lists and left space for another 24 innovative(!), new wonder(!) drugs urgently wanted by overenthusiastic specialist doctors.

b) The 45 essential drugs used at THC level were to be manufactured and/or sold under their generic names only.

c) A National Formulary incorporating all formulations of essential and supplementary drugs should be prepared and published not later than 1983.

d) Product patents in respect of pharmaceutical substances should not be allowed. Process patents could be allowed for a limited period if the basic substance only was manufactured within the country.

e) The Drugs Act of 1940 should be revised or replaced by new drug legislation with provision for: (i) a system of registration of all medicinal products including Ayurvedic, Unani and homeopathic medicines as these traditional medicines were not under the purview of the Drug Act; (ii) enforcement of good manufacturing practices; (iii) full control of labelling and advertisement; (iv) control of prices of finished drugs and raw materials; (v) prescription control of toxic/poisonous and habit-forming drugs;

(vi) summary trial for offences in special drug courts; (vii) heavy penalties including confiscation of equipment and properties for manufacture and/or selling of spurious and substandard drugs; (viii) departmental adjudication for fines of up to Taka 10,000; (ix) heavy penalties for possessing or selling drugs stolen from government stores, hospitals and dispensaries; (x) regulation of technology transfer and licensing agreements with foreign collaborators; (xi) restriction of ownership of retail pharmacies to professional pharmacists only; (xii) control of manufacture and sale of Unani, Ayurvedic and homeopathic drugs.

f) To ensure good manufacturing practice (GMP), each manufacturing company should employ qualified pharmacists. No manufacturer would be allowed to produce drugs without adequate quality control facilities. However, the small national drug manufacturers might be allowed to establish quality control laboratories on a collective basis.

g) A properly staffed and equipped National Drug Control Laboratory with appellate facilities should be set up as early as possible, not later than 1985. Besides quality testing this National Laboratory would develop appropriate standards and specifications for Unani and Ayurvedic drugs. It would help develop rational formulations as the market was flooded with irrational traditional medicines, many of them containing an alcohol content of over 40 per cent.

h) Multinational companies would not be allowed to manufacture simple products like common analgesics, vitamins, antacids etc. These were to be manufactured exclusively by local (national) firms.

i) The government was to control the prices of finished drugs as well as raw materials, packaging materials and intermediates. Raw and packaging materials of acceptable quality would be procured from international sources at competitive prices only. The maximum retail price (MRP) of finished drugs would be fixed on the basis of cost of production and reasonable profit. However, undue 'overhead' expenditure should be prevented. The Drug Administration was to be responsible for the control of pricing and its enforcement.

j) Arrangements should be made as early as possible to lease space within the campus of every government hospital up to THC level for private retail pharmacies under the supervision of qualified pharmacists to fill the prescriptions of qualified physicians at government-fixed prices. Training programmes for sales personnel in registered retail pharmacies should be undertaken on an emergency basis.

k) To strengthen the directorate of the Drug Administration (which had only 32 drug superintendents and inspectors in 1982 and had the impossible task of inspecting 177 manufacturing units, about 14,000 retail pharmacies and over 1,200 wholesalers), all Thana health administrators (who are qualified doctors with 7–10 years', experience) should be given a special course of training and be empowered to act as drug inspectors for the purpose of enforcement of necessary sanctions against retail pharmacies, wholesalers and pedlars of drugs at Thana level and below.

Notes

1. Planning Commission, Government of the People's Republic of Bangladesh, *The First Five Year Plan 1973–78*, Dhaka, November 1973.

2. Ibid.

3. Ibid.

4. Lall, Sanjaya, *The Multinational Corporation*, Macmillan, London, 1980.

5. McHenry, D. F. and Bird, K., 'Food Bungle in Bangladesh', *Foreign Policy*, No. 27, Summer 1977, quoted in Sen, A., *Poverty and Famines – An Essay on Entitlement and Deprivation*, Clarendon Press, Oxford, 1982.

6. Ministry of Health and Population Control, Government of the People's Republic of Bangladesh, Drugs Administration Section, No. S-DA/D-D-20/82/74, 27 April 1982.

7. The Haslemere Group, *Who Needs the Drug Companies?*, Haslemere Group, War on Want and Third World First Publications, London, undated but probably 1976.

8. Silverman, M. and Lee, P. R., *Pills, Profits and Politics*, University of California Press, Berkeley, 1974.

9. Silverman, M., *The Drugging of the Americas*, University of California Press, Berkeley, 1976.

10. WHO, *The Selection of Essential Drugs*, Technical Report Series 615, World Health Organization, Geneva, 1977.

11. Medawar, Charles, *Insult or Injury? An Enquiry into the Marketing and Advertising of British Food and Drug Products in the Third World*, Social Audit, London, 1979.

12. Public Citizen Health Research Group, *Pills That Do Not Work*, New York, 1980.

13. WHO, *The Selection of Essential Drugs*, Technical Report Series 641, World Health Organization, Geneva, 1979.

14. Dr Z. Sestak, WHO Programme Coordinator and Representative, letter to Dr Z. Chowdhury, A/3/43, 15 May 1982.

15. *The Pulse*, Dhaka, 9 May 1982.

16. Bibile, S./UNCTAD, *Case Studies in the Transfer of Technology: Pharmaceutical Policies in Sri Lanka*, UNCTAD Secretariat, United Nations, Geneva, June 1977.

17. UNCTAD, *Technology Policies in the Pharmaceutical Sector in Nepal*, Study prepared by Dr P. N. Suwal in co-operation with UNCTAD Secretariat, United Nations, Geneva, 1980.

18. A Thana is an administrative unit with an average population of 250,000. Bangladesh is divided into 464 Thanas. The term 'Thana', introduced during the British colonial administration, was renamed 'Upazila' (meaning sub-district) during the Ershad government. This was changed back to 'Thana' and the local government structure under 'Upazila' dismantled in 1992 by Khaleda Zia's government.

4

A storm unleashed

The Expert Committee worked intensively, taking over 1,000 man-hours to complete and submit the report to the Minister of Health on 11 May 1982. The report was approved by the Council of Ministers on 29 May 1982. Surprisingly, only a two-line news item on the National Drug Policy (NDP) was published next day as part of a standard, lengthy government communiqué on various matters. It went almost unnoticed. But when on 1 June 1982 the English-language daily, the *Bangladesh Times*, published the news as a lead item with the caption 'WHO prescription: only 248 basic drugs enough – 1,742 unnecessary drugs to be banned', the storm began.[1]

The same morning, Jane Abel Coon, the US ambassador to Bangladesh, called without prior appointment on the Chief Martial Law Administrator, General Ershad. Her mission was to convince him that as the policy was unacceptable to the USA it should not be implemented. She insisted that, at the very least, implementation of the policy should be postponed. General Ershad was new to the political arena and was perhaps unaware of the politics of aid and its close connections with the business interests of donor governments. Earlier, he had heard from a member of the Expert Committee how the US ambassador in Sri Lanka had issued an implied threat of withdrawal of food aid in 1975 because of the country's drug policy. He had been reluctant to believe this, seeing no reason why the USA should interfere in Sri Lanka's domestic policy, and now found himself equally astonished that the new drug policy formulated by Bangladesh should be a matter of concern to the USA. However, after Mrs Coon's visit, he was struck by the similarity between the two US ambassadors' attitudes and behaviour towards Third World governments.

In the afternoon of the same day, Shehabuddin Ahmed Nafa, the news reporter who had blown the whistle in the *Bangladesh Times*, was picked up by military security for questioning at army headquarters. He demanded to know why he was being interrogated as all he had done was to give front-page prominence to newly announced government policy. The interrogators, well-trained at the International Police Services School in Washington, DC (run by the Central Intelligence Agency – the CIA) were not amused. Nafa was released at midnight, after his colleagues had issued serious threats to stop publication of the next day's newspaper.

The question arises as to why such important news as the NDP was not properly published in all the newspapers. On the other hand, when a journalist, on his own initiative, gave proper coverage and credit to the government for following WHO recommendations, he found himself being harassed. There was no shortage of rumours about top police and security officials having been 'greased' by the drug industry to ensure that the story was suppressed.

The bribing of officials by industry is not an unusual event either in the Third World or in industrialised countries. According to Malcolm Baldrige, Secretary of Commerce in the Reagan Administration, small payments to foreign officials are not really bribes but 'grease' or 'facilitating payments'.[2] Facilitating payments are part of the US way of life. The drug industry, medical suppliers and their related membership associations gave US$1.85 million to influential Congressional candidates during the 1990 election campaign.[3] The issue is not about giving money to the best candidate, but about gaining access and influence. Since 'more and more medical decisions are being made on a political basis', the American Medical Association (AMA) raised US$4.7 million from its 65,000 members in one month and donated US$2.12 million to Congressional candidates in order to gain a platform for their point of view.[4] The Texas Medical Association's Political Action Committee spent US$1.3 million on state and federal elections for the same purpose. Senator John D. Rockefeller IV, a Democrat from West Virginia, received the highest amount both from the industry and from medical associations. Next came Henry Waxman, a Democrat from California, who happened to be the Chairman of the Senate's Health Subcommittee, Thad Cochran (Republican, Mississippi) and David Pryor (Democrat, Arkansas) who ran unopposed but received a large amount in contributions. Mike Synar, a Democrat from Oklahoma, was the only candidate who declined offers of 'facilitating contributions'.

In the days following the announcement of the Bangladesh National Drugs Policy, Mrs Coon had meetings with the editor of the most widely circulated Bengali daily, *Ittefaq*, the managing directors of US transnational companies and a number of other people to work out a strategy for preventing implementation of the policy. She also informed offices of the US Agency for International Development (USAID) in neighbouring countries about the dangers of a policy like NDP!

Much information about these meetings and communications is available under the US Freedom of Information Act. However, the

---

Confidential message, dated 2 June 1982, from Ambassador Coon to the Secretary of State in Washington, DC, with copies to the American embassies in Colombo, Calcutta, Islamabad, Karachi, Katmandu, New Delhi and Rangoon.

1. The Martial Law Administrator (MLA) has announced a new policy for the manufacture and sale of pharmaceuticals which significantly reduces the items which can be manufactured and sold in Bangladesh and impacts heavily on the multinational firms engaged in the sector. The new policy follows from a study of the sector by a special committee appointed by the MLA primarily from the government's medical administration and academia. According to the press release announcing the new policy, the committee tried to follow WHO guidelines and its review of British and European Pharmacopoeias and USP [US Pharmacopoeia]. The committee also studied pharmaceutical policy in Sri Lanka, Indonesia and Argentina.

2. The new policy specifically prohibits the manufacture and sale of 1,742 pharmaceutical products which are presently available in the country. With a few exceptions, it permits the manufacture and sale of 215 basic pharmaceuticals recommended by WHO for developing countries. Most of the prohibited drugs are tonics, lozenges, creams and a few liquid preparations with alcohol content, that are dangerous to children. Some preparations believed dangerous to children are permitted in tablet but not in liquid form.

3. The new policy also prohibits inter-party tolling arrangements for the manufacture of pharmaceuticals. Several major US firms now have these arrangements in Bangladesh under which a local firm manufactures its drug to standards established by an international firm which handles sales and distribution. In addition, the policy contains a list of preparations which can be manufactured by domestic firms but not by international pharmaceutical manufacturers located in Bangladesh.

4. Multinational firms have *secured an advance copy* [author's emphasis] of the full text which has not yet been released publicly. A preliminary study by a US firm indicates that it will lose approximately 25 per cent of the present revenues under the policy. The embassy will be consulting other pharmaceutical firms to assess the full impact of the new policy.

Point 5 of the document, on the meeting with General Ershad, was blacked out.

Source: Declassified document, Dacca/3598, 'New Drug Industry Policy', Department of State, A/CDC/MR, Washington DC, 13 January 1983.

details of Mrs Coon's conversations with General Ershad, various ministers and senior civil servants on a number of different dates remain classified until today, as do the names of the US embassy's

---

Confidential message sent in second week of June 1982 by Ambassador Coon to the Secretary of State in Washington, DC

1. Representatives of US pharmaceutical firms operating in Bangladesh have approached the embassy with requests for official support in resoslving this very controversial issue. US pharmaceutical firms with plants in Bangladesh include Squibb, Pfizer and SmithKline and French, the last of which is still under construction. In addition, Wyeth, American Cynamid and Upjohn have tolling arrangements with local pharmaceutical firms. There are also eight British, two West German and one Dutch pharmaceutical manufacturers, on tolling arrangements in Bangladesh.

2. A copy of the draft NDP we have received (...) recommends revision of the patent laws to eliminate product patents and to limit process patents, regulation of technology transfer and licensing arrangements, big provision of quality control facilities for small 'national' manufacturers, price controls at both input and retail levels with wholesale mark-ups based upon the cost of raw materials, and competitive international sourcing of inputs. In announcing this new policy the Advisor (minister) for Health also said that Bangladesh would immediately take the first steps in a gradual move toward generic labelling. Finally, some manufacturers have been told that they will be given one month to destroy raw materials intended for the manufacture of newly banned drugs. A possible confirmation of this is an announcement in the June 11 press requesting that all firms submit an inventory of such raw materials both in-country and in the order pipeline.

Comment: The mood of foreign investors in Dacca, larger Bangladeshi entrepreneurs and our Western diplomatic colleagues ranges from serious disappointment to anger. Just as the BDG [Bangladesh government] announced a new policy shifting most industrial emphasis to the private sector and welcoming foreign investment, it adopted this simplistic, populist-oriented pharmaceutical policy which will certainly give pause to any foreign investment and probably cause the domestic private sector to rethink investment proposals.

Another message sent from the US embassy in Dacca reported:

The British state that the investigation has already zeroed in on the British PVO [private voluntary organisation] Oxfam and the organisation's local collaborator Dr Zafrullah Chowdhury who was one of the Government's Expert Committee which drafted the policy.

Sources: Declassified documents, Dacca 3844 and 4022, A/CDC/MR, Department of State, Washington DC, 13 January 1983.

'excellent sources' in Bangladesh. Documents relating to the Bangladesh NDP obtained through the benefit of the Act show that one or two paragraphs in most documents have been blacked out. Release of the full documents was officially denied, and 'Release denied in part' was written on the documents.[5]

A public hearing

Transnational companies started mobilising the Bangladesh Medical Association (BMA) and elite public opinion. Many TNCs had retired army officers as their directors and administrators, who were able to brief the Martial Law Administration about what was happening. These pressures led General Ershad to order a public hearing, chaired by his principal staff officer, Major General Muzzammel Huq, which took place on 6 June 1982. It was attended by various representatives of TNCs and large national companies: Captain Rosslyn Bower, Managing Director of Squibb (Bangladesh) and a Vietnam veteran; Abdul Wahed, Managing Director of Fisons (Bangladesh); Farhad Ghuznavi, Managing Director of ICI (Bangladesh); and other members of Bangladesh Aushadh Shilpa Shamity (BASS – the Bangladesh Association of Pharmaceutical Industries). The hearing was also attended by members of Bangladesh Aushadh Prostutkarak Shamity (the Bangladesh Drug Manufacturers Association), an organisation of medium-sized and small pharmaceutical manufacturers, including Dr Ahmed Rafiq, a member of the BMA's Drug Evaluation Committee and General Manager of the Pakistani company Albert David.

The health minister, Dr Shamsul Huq, was present at the hearing, with all the members of the Expert Committee. He explained the rationale for the NDP and the criteria for evaluation of registered products, and also said that the Expert Committee would provide further clarification and explanation where needed.

The TNC representatives made no attempt to engage in a debate on the scientific rationale of the NDP. Instead, they insisted that generic-drugs policies had failed all over the world and that Bangladesh should remember what had happened to Zulfiquar Ali Bhutto, who had tried to introduce generic drugs in Pakistan, hinting that this policy had played a role in his downfall. They protested that Bangladesh was attempting to ban drugs widely available elsewhere; as an example they cited gripe water and pointed out that Woodward's Gripe Water was a household name in Britain. To this, the committee replied that there was no mention of gripe water in any of the textbooks on paediatrics, including those published in Britain.

Echoing the US ambassador, the TNC representatives called for the implementation of the proposed NDP to be delayed, pending a review by an independent body. Arguing that the policy would deter foreign investors, they made a veiled threat of withdrawing from Bangladesh.

The small companies took a more reasonable approach. Realising that 90 per cent of their products had no scientific validity, they complained that if the Drug Administration had had doubts about the efficacy of their products it should not have permitted their production in the first place, and that its negligence was now going to ruin them financially. They urged that in future the Drug Control Committee should approve or reject new products within two months of applications for registration being submitted. They also said that they should be allowed to manufacture and sell Schedule II and III drugs for the next two years and finally, to compensate for their loss, that they should be given easy credit.

The TNCs fired the final shot. BASS pointed out: 'These harmful medicines were approved by the Recipe Committee of which Professor Nurul Islam, Director of the Institute of Postgraduate Medicine and Research, is the Chairman. Professor Islam is also the Chairman of the Expert Committee.' They concluded that the recommendations of the Expert Committee were 'suicidal'.[6] As it was a fact that Professor Islam was the Chairman of both committees, he had no defence. In all, the meeting lasted for over three hours.

Major General Muzzamel Huq reported later that before the public hearing the drug manufacturers had met with senior officials of the army and the civil administration and with members of the Council of Ministers and had succeeded in making almost everybody believe that the NDP was a ludicrous policy with no scientific basis. However, during the public hearing he had realised that the TNCs' campaign was based on total falsehood and that they were simply wielding their power in defence of their commercial interests. He recommended that the policy should immediately be given a legal framework.

On 7 June 1982, the health minister made the NDP document public. That evening, Rosslyn Bower, John Quinn, Commercial Officer at the British High Commission, and Gordon Powers, Acting Deputy Chief of the US Mission in Bangladesh, held a meeting at the home of Mr Bower.[7] Gordon Powers was widely known at the time as the CIA contact person in Bangladesh, working under cover as Economic Counsellor in the US Embassy.

Bower reported on a meeting which he had had with the Bangladesh government that morning. The documents on this meeting show that the manufacturers and the US Embassy had heard from their 'excellent sources' that the Council of Ministers had decided to put off decisions about details of the NDP until mid-July.[8]

Gordon Powers expressed the opinion that the Bangladesh government 'might be more receptive to an approach pointing to the conflict between the pharmaceutical policy and the industrial policy and to a suggestion that [it] would be unilaterally breaking both written and implied contracts with international firms than to any form of attack on the new policy'.[9]

On the same day, in another part of the globe, at the State Department, Washington, DC, George Bush, then US Vice-President, opened a two-day meeting of the International Federation of Pharmaceutical Manufacturers Associations (IFPMA), attended by 300 industrialists from 22 countries. He stated: 'The growth of federal regulation affects the pharmaceutical industry perhaps as much as any other' and reassured the audience that the Reagan Administration would 'end this adverse relationship'. Dr Halfdan Mahler, Director-General of WHO, was also present at this meeting. He told the drug company executives: 'If you are not the devils that some people would describe you as, permit me to say, very quietly, that you are not angels either. Some of your promotional practices in the developing countries are perhaps excessive and some of your double standards of marketing are perhaps dubious.'[10]

The next day, General Ershad had an unexpected invitation from the White House to visit the USA. For the rulers of Third World countries such an invitation is viewed as recognition of their governments.

Fact and fiction

The TNCs and the US ambassador were successful in persuading the pro-US *Ittefaq-New Nation* group of newspapers to make bleak forecasts concerning the NDP. The *New Nation* reported: 'The new drug policy would lead to the closure of many medicine factories, making thousands jobless. Production of medicine will fall by up to 80 per cent if the drug policy is implemented.'[11]

The industry-financed weekly, *The Pulse*, reported similar statements, ignoring the warning of the Martial Law Authority that rumour-mongers would be severely dealt with, receiving a sentence of seven years' imprisonment. Newspapers would not have had the courage to ignore this warning without the assurance from somebody high up in the army that they could do so with impunity.

Concerned about these reports, the health minister, Dr Shamsul Huq, had a long meeting with members of the Expert Committee. The committee's analysis showed the reports to have been fabricated by the anti-drug policy lobby, which was concerned with the financial health of the drug companies rather than the physical health of the people. Members of the committee argued that other newspapers had not yet commented adversely on the policy, and neither the drug companies nor the pro-TNC newspapers had ever questioned the scientific validity of the policy. They reiterated that the essential drugs concept was promoted by the World Health Organization with the aim of serving the people better and expressed the conviction that the national pharmaceutical industry would in fact flourish in the future under such a dynamic policy. However, for this to happen, the government needed to make a special effort to educate the public, as well as doctors and medical students, about the concept of essential drugs, first by dispelling the fear which the various newspaper reports and the whispering campaign had created, and second by showing them that better treatment was available with effective drugs at cheaper prices.

The committee members also pointed out that the newspapers which had published the reports must have had the assured support of some influential members of the government; in saying this they were particulary referring to Brigadier Chishty, Director of Information and Security.

Draft policy made law

The Council of Ministers had participated with unusual vigour in a second discussion on the National Drug Policy on the evening of 11 June, chaired by General Ershad. The finance minister, A. M. A. Muhith, and the industry minister, Mohammad Shaiful Azam, voiced the sentiments of TNCs, stating that the introduction of the policy was premature as it would frighten away foreign investors. Interestingly, both Muhith and Shaiful Azam were from the erstwhile Pakistan civil service. Later on, Muhith was absorbed in the World Bank. Dr Huq pleaded the case for the NDP well and insisted that General Ershad sign the legal document for the NDP, the Drug (Control) Ordinance 1982, before leaving for the USA. According to

Dr Huq, General Ershad paused for a while and then signed the document.[12] General Ershad left for the USA the next day.

Dr Huq ensured that the news was flashed on Bangladesh radio and television the same night. An Extraordinary Gazette of the Bangladesh government was published on 12 June by the Ministry of Law and Land Reforms.[13] At the end of the document were two significant statements: 'These lists [Schedules I, II, and III] are not absolute. According to the criteria laid down there may be some addition or deletion of products from any category.'[14]

On 16 June, Lewis A. Engman, President of the US Pharmaceutical Manufacturers Association (PMA) wrote a three-page letter to General Ershad (Appendix 1) in which he warned of the 'negative impact' that the new policy could have on health care in Bangladesh and pointed out that several provisions of the new policy, including the 'excessively rigid interpretation of the concept of an essential drugs list', had already been 'tried and rejected' in countries such as Sri Lanka and Pakistan. Quoting Dr Sanjaya Lall, a well-known critic of TNCs, on the adverse effects of a similar policy in India, Engman lamented: 'It would be particularly unfortunate if Bangladesh, which has made such impressive progress in recent years, were to follow the mistaken pharmaceutical policies of such countries.' Finally, he proposed to General Ershad that the implementation of the policy be delayed, and that as the 'issues at hand' were 'vital both to the well-being of the people of Bangladesh and to the investment climate in your country', a review panel to include delegates selected by and from the Bangladesh Medical Association, the Bangladesh Pharmaceutical Society and the Bangladesh Association of Pharmaceutical Industries be formed to 'study the matter in depth'.[15]

A meeting between General Ershad and the PMA was arranged to take place during the former's visit to the USA. The US embassy in Bangladesh soon learnt of this and sent another memo to the State Department: 'Industry sources in Dacca state that a meeting has been arranged in New York between General Ershad and officials of the PMA. Embassy would appreciate any read-out from the meeting.'[16]

General Ershad's visit to the USA was extremely important for him. He met President Reagan on 18 June. Later he met Vice-President George Bush, with whom he agreed to a review of the Bangladesh National Drug Policy. General Ershad also said, in response to George Bush's suggestion, that he would welcome a visit to Bangladesh by independent US scientists to advise him on the policy. What he did not realise was that George Bush was a director of the seventh-largest US transnational company, Eli Lilly, and had substantial shares in other drug companies.

Meanwhile, the oldest and most prestigious medical journal, *The Lancet*, published simultaneously in London (UK) and Baltimore (USA), made a very pertinent observation on Bangladesh's drug policy on 19 June 1982: 'The power of the transnational is great and the stakes are high. In the past, governments and their ministers have sometimes yielded to pressure. If the government [of Bangladesh] brings its new policy to fruition the message will not be lost on other parts of the third world.'[17]

Increasing pressure

Dr Shamsul Huq requested the Bangladesh Medical Association (BMA) several times to organise a meeting with the Expert Committee. This the BMA flatly refused to do. Moreover, they told the minister that products such as cough mixtures, alkali preparations, gripe water, enzyme and vitamin liquids, antipyretic analgesic novalgin, and antidiarrhoeal preparations were not banned anywhere else in the world, ignoring the fact that the production and sale of vitamin syrups in 15 ml bottles with droppers were permitted under the policy. They also maintained that the national drug industry would be ruined, since most local companies prepared only liquid preparations, and that manufacturers of glass bottles and tamper-proof caps, as well as the printing and packaging industries, would also be seriously affected. The BMA's concern was echoed in a BASS advertisement entitled 'An appeal to Martial Law Authority', which appeared in all national dailies on 23 June 1982, coinciding with General Ershad's return from the USA.

This kind of mutually beneficial alliance between the drug industry and medical associations had already been shown by Kefauver,[18] Sainsbury[19] and Hathi[20] to exist in the USA, the UK and India. Similar alliances have also been demonstrated in Canada[21] and the Philippines.[22]

The Bangladesh government started facing the heat of increasing pressure. TNCs continued to lobby the elite, the politicians and the newspapers. The media played a crucial role in the campaign against the NDP. *The Pulse* wrote: 'The treatment prescribed by the Expert Committee reminds one of the classic phrase, "The operation was a success but the patient died". In this case, unfortunately, the patient is not only the pharmaceutical industry alone, but the whole economic structure of the country.'[23]

Most of the major national dailies and weeklies started publishing reports against the National Drug Policy which were prepared and circulated by BASS. Despite their pessimistic tone, these articles helped create an awareness of the controversy among the people, who started showing an interest in learning about the other side of the story. Gonoshasthaya Kendra (GK) and the Consumers Association of Bangladesh asked the BMA to supply the names and addresses of its members, so that they could send them publications on the rationale of a drug policy. The request was turned down.[24]

Drug company representatives campaigned vigorously against the NDP, lobbying successfully in various constituencies. They encouraged doctors to see the policy as a curb on their right to prescribe and an infringement of their clinical freedom. TNC manoeuvrings resulted in 23 professors and 40 senior doctors presenting a petition to the BMA President on 30 July, demanding disciplinary action against Professor Nurul Islam and Dr Zafrullah Chowdhury for their active role in the propagation of the NDP and for 'maligning' the medical profession through their writings in support of the policy. They threatened to resign from the BMA if serious action were not taken against these two individuals.

A number of professors and associate professors of Dacca Medical College and Sir Salimullah Medical College signed the petition. Notable names were: Professor Mohammed Yusuf Ali (Fellow of the Royal College of Physicians); Professor Maniruzzaman (Fellow of the Royal College of Surgeons, FRCS); Professor Firoza Begum (Fellow of the Royal College of Obstetricians and Gynaecologists); Professor S. G. M. Chowdhury (FRCP); Professor M. Q. Huq (Member of the Royal College of Physicians, MRCP); Professor Mirza M. Islam (FRCS); Professor Abu Ahmed Chowdhury (FRCS); Professor Maleka Begum, (Diploma in Child Health, MRCP [Paediatrics]); Associate Professor M. A. Hadi (Fellow of the College of Physicians and Surgeons).[25]

Other sections of the public had misgivings about the policy. Intellectuals were confused by the suddenness of the decision to implement a new policy, unexpected from a military government. The urban elite were annoyed as their favourite digestive enzymes, tonics, elixirs and cough mixtures were banned. Mothers were angered by the banning of gripe water. Unfortunately, the government did nothing to allay their fears and correct misinformation.

As a response to the confusion created by TNCs and to the government's sudden silence and failure to promote the NDP, a new consumer organisation, Sabar Janya Shasthaya (Health for All, or

HFA) was established by a group of politically conscious physicians, lawyers, journalists, women activists, freedom fighters and university teachers to promote health education and to publicise the other side of the story. Advertisements and booklets produced by HFA in support of the drug policy had a tremendous reception. Apart from a few Dhaka daily newspapers and weeklies, other newspapers around the country eagerly published features written by HFA on the role of TNCs in various countries and the preponderance of useless drugs even in the West.

High-level manoeuvrings

The drug companies did not simply confine themselves to publishing their propaganda in newspapers and spreading rumours among the medical profession and members of the elite. They pulled other strings too. British, Dutch and West German ambassadors called on General Ershad to express their dismay at the proposed drug policy. The West German ambassador was particulary angry and said that the policy would deter German investment in the country. He said that, the German TNC Hoechst had intended to expand in Bangladesh but was now reluctant to do so.

This was not the first time that Germany had sided with its drug companies operating in other countries. Germany is grateful to its pharmaceutical companies for their contribution to rebuilding the country after the Second World War. Following the defeat of Germany and the Axis forces, the Allied forces dismantled all major industries in Germany on the grounds of their involvement in arms production. However, because of US economic interests, Germany's chemical industry survived this onslaught, although the giant IG Farben was broken into smaller companies: Hoechst, BASF, Bayer and Aniline Fabrikation – the ancestor of Agfa. Hoechst and Bayer soon became among the largest pharmaceutical companies in the world, contributing greatly to the German economy.[26]

When two members of the medical faculty of Dar es Salaam University circulated a paper criticising the German company Asta Werke for marketing in Africa a drug which was banned in the UK and USA for safety reasons, the West German embassy sent a warning letter to the University, reminding them of their dependence on German aid for the construction of a new engineering school.[27]

The British threat was more subtle. The foreign secretary, Douglas Hurd, said in the UK House of Commons: 'We are keen that the Bangladesh Government should use its scarce resources wisely. We are also keen that they should succeed in their policy of encouraging foreign investment to help them with the development of an industrial economy. We, in common with other Western governments, have explained this to the Bangladesh Government through our High Commission in Dhaka. It is important that in trying to achieve the aims of the pharmaceutical policy they do not discriminate against foreign-owned manufacturing companies in Bangladesh and do not frighten off prospective foreign investors.'[28]

On 24 June 1982, the US State Department had a meeting with the PMA. This was attended by Leonard A. Holbrook of the PMA, Walter Wein of Wyeth, Meric L. Legnim of SmithKline Beecham, M. William Roche of Pfizer and Robert J. Paulus of Squibb.

The meeting reviewed the basic points that the NDP would 'damage health standards' and 'increase smuggling, due to the continuing need for drugs' and stated that the proposed measures 'would make infeasible the continued presence of virtually all MNC companies [multinational companies]'.[29] The State Department informed the meeting that Ambassador Jane Coon had already mentioned these concerns to General Ershad and that the embassy officer Gordon Powers had been pursuing the matter.[30]

The PMA informed the State Department that they had had a meeting in New York with the Bangladesh foreign minister, A. R. S. Doha, who had been non-committal but had suggested a US team '[came] out to talk'. Finally, it was decided that the embassy in Bangladesh should be formally instructed 'to send aide-memoires outlining earlier points and passing along a PMA letter'. The meeting noted: *'PMA will draft both'* [author's emphasis].

Ambassador Coon was in Washington from 7 to 13 July and met the PMA on 12 July. In accordance with the strategy decided by the meeting, the Secretary of State instructed the US embassy in Bangladesh to express concern over the drug policy at the highest government levels.

The behaviour of the USA towards Bangladesh may be compared with its behaviour towards the Philippines. When the Philippines National Drug Policy (PNDP) was announced by President Corazon Aquino in April 1987, two US Senators – Allan Cranston, a Democrat from California, and Richard Lugar, a Republican from Indiana, who were major sponsors of a mini Marshall Plan to support development of the Philippines with a very substantial aid package – wrote to President Aquino, advising her that the task of stimulating new US investments could become 'more difficult' if a national drug policy were implemented. The US State Department also exerted pressure. It urged the Philippines government to implement the Generic Law 'in as non-discriminatory and non-compulsory manner as possible ... to avoid serious damage to the Philippines' reputation as a place to invest'.[31] The US ambassador in Manila also warned the Philippine health minister that the drug policy would discourage foreign investment.

The first review of the National Drug Policy

Pressure on General Ershad yielded results. A Review Committee consisting of six army doctors was formed on 6 July 1982. Major General A. R. Khan, a consultant physician and Director-General of the Armed Forces Medical Services, was appointed its chairman. There were two particularly vocal members. One was Colonel Anis Waiz, a consultant physician at the Combined Military Hospital, Dhaka, whose brother Mamun Waiz was the commercial manager of Bangladesh Pharmaceutical Industry (BPI), a joint venture of the French TNC Rhone Poulenc and the Bangladesh government. The other was Colonel Shahjahan Hafiz, a medical administrator and the brother-in-law of M. R. Siddiqui, a former Minister of Industry and Bangladesh's ambassador to the USA during Sheikh Mujibur's time. At the time of the review, M. R. Siddiqui was the managing director of Therapeutics, a medium-sized national company which had a third-party licensing agreement with Wyeth, a US trans-national drug company. He was also Chairman of the Bangladesh Chamber of Commerce.

Other members of the Review Committee were Brigadier M. R. Chowdhury, Commandant of the Army Pathology Laboratory; Colonel A. M. Khan, Director of Medical Services for the Bangladesh Navy; and Colonel Ramizud Din Ahmed, Director of the Army Medical Services.

The US 'scientific committee'

The US ambassador, Jane Abel Coon, informed Dr Shamsul Huq that a four-member 'independent scientific committee' would be arriving in Dhaka on 20 July 1982 to examine the drug policy and advise the Bangladesh government. When the health minister asked for the curriculum vitae of each of these experts, the US ambassador was furious, implying that it was impertinent for a minister of a Third World country to ask for the CVs of experts from the USA. She most discourteously left the minister without having tea, which had already been laid on the table. But before leaving she informed him that the 'independent scientific committee' had been agreed by General Ershad during his visit to the US, a fact of which the health minister had previously been unaware. However, when Dr Huq contacted the Expert Committee, they insisted that they must have the CVs of the experts from the USA to enable them to prepare a strategy to face them. The health minister persisted with his request for the CVs, which were finally made available.

The members of the so-called 'scientific committee' were: Leonard A. Holbrook, Far East Regional Director, International Division, PMA; Lafayette Kirbin, Vice-President, Squibb; Dr Edmund Maar, Director of Research and Development, Wyeth Laboratories; and Walter Wein, Special Assistant to the vice-president of Wyeth Laboratories. Not one of them was an independent scientist. One was a quality control manager, two were marketing managers and the fourth was a public relations officer!

General Ershad later told the health minister that when he had agreed to an independent advisory committee he had expected it to consist of officials from the US Food and Drug Administration and members of the National Academy of Sciences and other academics, but definitely not representatives from the pharmaceutical industry.

On 20 July, General Ershad had a meeting with his Council of Ministers and zonal martial law administrators. The industry minister, Shaiful Azam, asked General Ershad persistently to reconsider the NDP in the light of the losses that would be incurred by TNCs and the impact of terminating toll manufacturing licences. General Ershad retorted that the drug companies were bleeding the people of Bangladesh and had made quite enough profits to be able to incur some losses.

The US 'independent scientific committee' met executives from drug companies and from BASS and also had a few meetings with the Bangladesh Medical Association and the Review Committee. They did not wish to meet the members of the Expert Committee. The report of their findings was never made public.

The Review Committee interviewed representatives of the national drug industry, TNCs, BASS, the Chemists and Druggists Association, the Chamber of Commerce and the BMA. It also met separately with the former president of the BMA, Professor Firoza Begum, who was a director of Pfizer and owned shares in three other drug companies. The BMA's statement was submitted to the Review Committee by the former general secretary of the BMA, Dr Sarwar

Ali, a member of the Central Committee of the Communist Party of Bangladesh and Assistant Medical Director of Pfizer (Bangladesh).

The Expert Committee, on its own initiative, met the Review Committee and enquired whether they wanted explanations on any point in the NDP. The Review Committee politely declined the offer and said that they had a copy of the NDP, which was self-explanatory.

'Ignorance or partisanship'

The Review Committee submitted its report, alongside submissions from various other groups, direct to General Ershad on 12 August. Although the submissions from BASS and the BMA were made separately, they bore strange similarities. The BMA submitted that combination antiobiotics were safe; that drugs such as Novalgin (dipyrone) and Mexaform/Enterovioform (clioquinol) were effective in reducing pain and controlling diarrhoea; that children needed tetracycline syrup, Orabolin drops (an anabolic steroid) and Periactin (cyproheptadine); and that cough mixtures, alkali mixture (supposedly to prevent blood and urine becoming acid) and gripe water had been used for many years without any problem; and that adverse reactions and side-effects were rare and occurred only in cases of self-prescription. The BMA concluded that the problem lay not in the drugs themselves but in the unrestricted availability of these drugs without prescription. Therefore, the only policy measure the government should undertake was to ensure that these drugs were available on prescription only. The BMA did not use a single generic name in its submission.

The Review Committee's document is a travesty of an objective report, revealing at best ignorance and at worst outright partisanship.

On 14 August, a one-and-a-half-page, highly emotive advertisement by BASS appeared in all the major Bengali daily newspapers with the headline, 'Crisis in Drug Industry: A Practical Analysis by Bangladesh Ausadh Shilpa Shamity'.[32] It claimed there was an international conspiracy by 'Christian' donor agencies such as Oxfam and War on Want and their local partners to destroy Muslim Bangladesh. The same advertisement appeared in all the major English-language dailies on 22 August.[33]

The advertisement also questioned the role of Gonoshasthaya Kendra, cleverly playing with words to insinuate that Gonoshasthaya Pharmaceutical Ltd was owned by NOVIB, the Dutch aid agency providing grants to Third World voluntary organisations. BASS tried to portray NOVIB as a Dutch business competing with British and

US TNCs. Rumours were also rife that Indian pharmaceutical products had flooded the market.

Strengthened by the Review Committee's report, both the drug industry and the foreign embassies increased the pressure on General Ershad to abandon the NDP. The London *Guardian* wrote: 'A major confrontation between multinational pharmaceutical manufacturers and the military government of Bangladesh is shaping up. If Bangladesh wins, it will be the first country to successfully implement a World Health Organization resolution to eliminate dangerous and useless drugs from the market and to make useful drugs less expensive.'[34]

US citizens challenge their government

Although Bangladesh's drug policy was opposed by the US government, it received unexpected support from US citizens.

The international pharmaceutical bi-weekly journal *Scrip* published the news of US pressure on the Bangladesh government to delay the implementation of the new drug policy in its issue of 21 July. The news had drawn the attention of Ralph Nader, the famous public rights crusader, as well as concerned US citizens, consumer bodies, the Interfaith Center on Corporate Responsibility, various church groups and human rights activists. These individuals and organisations expressed their support for the Bangladesh NDP and started raising questions about US opposition to the policy with their senators, congressmen and the State Department. Many of them reminded the State Department of the US government's expression of support for WHO's Action Programme on Essential Drugs at the 35th World Health Assembly (WHA) held in May 1982. On critical examination of the WHA documents, the State Department noted that Professor Arthur Hull Hayes, Commissioner of the US Food and Drug Administration, had made a statement at the World Health Assembly on 10 May 1982.[35]

Professor Hayes had said on this occasion that the United States had taken an active role in the development of the essential drugs programme and was pleased to see that the report of the ad hoc committee contained proposals which could be developed into an effective programme. All delegates appreciated the need for the people of *all countries* to have access to pharmaceutical products that were relevant to their health needs and *priced within their means* [my emphasis]: that need was particularly acute in developing countries. The Action Programme on Essential Drugs had the potential for helping countries meet their needs, and the United States strongly supported it.

The State Department was intrigued to find in WHA documents that Mohammed Siddiqur Rahman, Secretary of Health and Population Control for the Bangladesh government, had made no mention of forthcoming action in the pharmaceutical sector in Bangladesh when he expressed support at the WHA for WHO's Action Programme on Essential Drugs and spoke of the need of Third World countries to obtain cheaper drugs and become self-reliant in the production and supply of drugs.

Dr Sidney M. Wolfe and Benjamin Gordon of the Public Citizen Health Research Group in Washington wrote to the health minister, Shamsul Huq on 9 August: 'We support your goals and the policies designed to protect the health and welfare of your citizens, and we hope you will take further steps in this direction.'[36]

Referring to the removal of harmful, dangerous and ineffective drugs from the Bangladesh market, they wrote, 'Many of these drugs were removed from the US market during the past twelve years on the recommendation of eminent medical scientists; many of the drug mixtures you are removing were deemed to be "irrational combinations" by the former Committee on Drugs of the American Medical Association and their use was "not recommended".'[37] Referring to economic considerations, they said, 'The ... measures you have adopted to encourage the development of a viable domestic drug manufacturing industry have been adopted by most if not all industrialized countries in the form of tariffs, quotas and subsidies.'[38]

The Public Citizen Health Research Group also wrote to George Schultz, the US Secretary of State, on 18 August: 'To pressure the Bangladesh Government to delay the withdrawal from the market of dangerous, ineffective, useless or unnecessarily expensive drugs is unconscionable. ... Many of these drugs have been removed from the US market in recent years or were found to be irrational by eminent scientists.'[39]

Referring to the Bangladesh government's decision not to allow TNCs to manufacture and market oral vitamins and antacids, two out of over 250 products, the group asked Mr Shultz: 'Is it not hypocritical for us to protect many of our domestic industries from foreign competition by tariffs, quotas and subsidies while at the same time protesting against Bangladesh's program to develop a domestic drug industry?'[40] It further raised the question: 'Can you imagine the indignation and outrage on the part of the American people if the British, French, German or any government would ask us to delay a decision of our authorities to remove undesirable drugs from the market here?'[41]

On 19 August the *Washington Post* published a front-page news story entitled 'US is aiding Drug Companies in Bangladesh'[42] which reported that the US Government was putting pressure on the Bangladesh Government to delay implementation of the new drug policy. It quoted a government spokesman as saying: 'The State Department has a statutory responsibility for assisting American interests abroad. In this particular case, the US government is also concerned that these regulations may inhibit future foreign investment in Bangladesh.'[43]

On the same day, the State Department made a rejoinder which brought to the surface the collusion of the Bangladesh Medical Association and certain government officials, both civil and military, with the TNCs and the American Embassy in Bangladesh. The State Department declared: 'The US government has not brought "pressure" on the government of Bangladesh to reconsider its new drug policy. Members of the health care profession in Bangladesh and a number of Bangladesh government officials have expressed concern over what they view as the precipitous [sic] way in which the ordinance was promulgated and over the limited participation of the health care community in Bangladesh in formulating the ordinance. In light of the concern in Bangladesh, the government of Bangladesh *on its own initiative* [my emphasis] has undertaken to review the ordinance before final implementation.'[44]

In another internal document, the State Department said: 'After consultation with the pharmaceutical companies and on instruction, Ambassador Coon made representations to several ministers with the purpose of facilitating contacts between the GOB [Government of Bangladesh] and US firms. ... She noted the policy would discourage investment by, inter alia, not affording national treatment, and suggested that implementation of the policy be delayed and reviewed by a panel of interested experts. *A joint demarche with other concerned countries (UK, FRG, Netherlands and Switzerland) was also made* [my emphasis], and PMA representatives journeyed to Dacca to make similar points.'[45]

In response to Senator Mathias Jr's query, the State Department again denied applying pressure on the Bangladesh Government and said, 'The Bangladesh Government of its *own accord* [my emphasis] has undertaken to review the ordinance with a wider spectrum of concerned parties before final implementation, an action which the US Government supports.'[46]

Similarly, in its response to Dr Wolfe of the Public Citizen Health Research Group, the State Department said that 'consistent with State Department policy' the Embassy in Dhaka had 'facilitated a dialogue between the Bangladesh Government and the pharmaceutical industry, while expressing the *hope* [my emphasis] that the Bangladesh Government might delay implementation while both domestic and international firms had an opportunity to discuss the ordinance with the Bangladesh Government. *Other concerned governments* [my emphasis] made similar approaches.'[47]

Dr Wolfe replied, 'Imagine the outrage of the US public if a foreign government asked us to delay implementing a health-protecting decision of our Food and Drug Administration or the Environmental Protection Agency! Moreover, it is rather naive to ignore that Bangladesh is a US aid recipient and that a "hope" expressed by our State Department is perceived as a threat, veiled or unexpressed though it may be.'[48]

It is not only in the Third World that the US government interferes with the domestic policies of sovereign countries. It has occasionally tried to twist the arm of industrialised countries too. When President Reagan met the Canadian Prime Minister Brian Mulroney in March 1983 he discussed the question of Canadian drug patents, as these had been described by his chief trade advisor, Ed Pratt, who was also the president of Pfizer, as 'trade irritants'. Vice-President George Bush publicly complained about the delay in the promised changes when he visited Canada in June 1986.[49] Finally, in December 1987, the conservative Mulroney government passed an amendment to the existing patent law which effectively destroyed the main benefit of compulsory licensing.

National and international support

Support for the NDP also came from certain quarters in the UK. Laurie Pavit, a British MP and a former chairman of the Parliamentary Labour Party Health Group, wrote to the Bangladesh health minister, 'I wish to add my voice to those who applaud the action of the Government of Bangladesh in adopting a national drug policy on behalf of the people of Bangladesh.' He also wrote, 'Having myself lived in India I believe the policy you have introduced can only be to the benefit of the population and I warmly congratulate the Government on its positive and progressive decision.'[50]

The London *Guardian* commented: 'The military government of Bangladesh has at a stroke done something that no other developing country or developed one for that matter has dared to do – it has enacted, almost in its entirety, the World Health Assembly's resolution on essential drugs. This draconian act has been interpreted as a massive assault on the multinational companies that dominate the country's drug market. In fact, it should mean that many more Bangladeshis will get the drugs they really need at a price the country can afford.'[51] Support also came from the *New Statesman* of London, in an article by Amrit Wilson, 'Dacca curbs drugs companies', on 9 July 1982.

On 8 August , the *Sunday Times* published a news story about the pressure exerted by TNCs and the US government on Bangladesh to delay the implementation of the new drug policy and to give in to 'a solution acceptable to both sides'. The article also mentioned the forthcoming visit to Bangladesh by 'a group of scientific experts' and commented that these 'experts' were no more than the representatives of US companies and the PMA. *The Economist* commented: 'American drug makers are afraid that Bangladesh could set a trend which would cut sharply into this $30 billion a year market.'[52]

Congratulatory letters and telegrams to the Bangladesh government from churches, non-governmental organisations (NGOs), scientists, social scientists, doctors and academics from countries in the North and the South started pouring in.

Unexpected support for the drug policy came from progressive intellectuals in Bangladesh when, on 4 August 1982, important members of the Dhaka University Teachers Association (DUTA) and a number of physicians and journalists made a statement in the press that the NDP was a pro-people policy and would bring practical benefit to the people of Bangladesh if implemented fully. They called upon the government to inform all concerned professions about the scientific reasons for banning various kinds of medicines. However, they expressed doubts about whether the military government would carry the policy through and suspected it might be just trying to 'bluff' the people.[53] Interestingly, DUTA had been the first organisation to hold a protest march against the military government soon after the coup in March 1982.

Among 229 notable signatories were: Professor Ahmed Sharif, Professor Kabir Chowdhury, Dr Emajuddin (present vice-chancellor of Dacca University), Dr Maniruzzaman Mia (a former vice-chancellor of Dacca University and the then president of DUTA) and Professor Saaduddin, all of various departments of Dhaka University; Professor Mahbubullah (presently pro-vice-chancellor of National University) and Professor Hayat Hossain from Chittagong

University; well-known journalists such as Enayetullah Khan, editor of the left-leaning English weekly *Holiday*, Santosh Gupta of the *Daily Sangbad*, Nirmal Sen of the *Daily Bangla*, Habibur Rahman Milon of the daily *Ittefaq*; Aziz Misir, freelance writer and film critic, and Dr Monwar Hossain, chairman of the Bangladesh Institute of Development Studies. All of these were highly respected names in Bangladesh.

On 21 August, General Ershad asked the external Publicity Department of the Ministry of Foreign Affairs to circulate copies of an article from the *Washington Post* of 19 August, entitled 'US is Aiding Drug Companies in Bangladesh'; this exposed the US government's interference and pressure.

Review Committee versus Expert Committee

The Review Committee's report was diametrically opposed to that of the Expert Committee. Following a suggestion from a member of the Expert Committee, General Ershad decided to bring the two committees face to face in an attempt to establish the scientific validity or otherwise of their reports. This session was held on 7 September 1982, in the President's Meeting Room.

The meeting was like a courtroom battle, with General Ershad in the chair. The Expert Committee appeared, with current editions of *Pharmacology*, the British and US pharmacopoeia, relevant journals and the latest edition of WHO's *The Selection of Essential Drugs*. It also brought slides, projectors and even multi-plugs and extension cables! The debate lasted five hours. The presentation convinced General Ershad of the scientific validity of the NDP.

However, the time allowed for reformulation of Schedule II drugs was extended to one year and that for utilisation of Schedule III drugs to 18 months. No extension was given for Schedule I drugs but loperamide and five other dental antiseptics with 5–10 per cent alcohol content were taken off the proscribed list. Thirty-three drugs produced under third-party licence were permitted until the expiry of the contracts. Fifty-five other drugs manufactured by 52 small national companies were placed in a new schedule with a two-year allowance. After these adjustments, the final list of banned drugs stood at 1,666.

Shortly afterwards, the health secretary, M. Siddiqur Rahman, was suddenly replaced by A. B. M. Ghulam Mustafa, a civil servant well known for his support of the pharmaceutical industry and another member of the former elite civil service of Pakistan. Ghulam

Mustafa had a direct interest in two of the largest traditional medicine manufacturing plants. He was the government-nominated director on the boards of Bangladesh Pharmaceutical Industry, Hoechst, and Fisons. Mustafa's nephew owned two of the three largest Ayurvedic manufacturing companies, in which it was alleged that Mustafa and his brother had 25 per cent shares.

Traditional medicines reviewed

Manufacturers of Ayurvedic and Unani medicines, taking advantage of the loopholes in the old drug legislation, and in response to market demand, started producing banned allopathic drugs such as gripe water, alkalis and cough mixtures. To prevent them producing allopathic medicines and to apply the NDP criteria to Ayurvedic, Unani and homeopathic medicines, a 13-member expert committee was formed on 27 February 1983, with Dr Nurul Anwar, Director of the Drug Administration, as its convener. Three experts on each type of traditional medicine were included in the committee.

The committee asked all traditional manufacturers to submit information about their manufacturing plants, premises and formulations. It received 76,434 formulations from 1,330 manufacturers. Upon investigation, the committee was able to verify the existence of 270 manufacturers, mostly functioning with primitive and crude facilities. The committee also discovered 16 registered and a few dozen unregistered distilleries producing alcohol, attached to Ayurvedic manufacturing plants. These manufacturers were producing over 25,000 brands of traditional medicine. The committee recommended only 431 medicines.

The committee also found that homeopathic medicines have an alcohol content of between 10 and 20 per cent while many Ayurvedic medicines contain over 40 per cent ethyl alcohol. The committee recommended that no medicine, whether homeopathic, Unani or Ayurvedic, should have an alcohol content of more than 5 per cent, in accordance with the principle laid down in the NDP. The committee submitted its report to the Drug Control Committee on 20 October 1983, as per provision of the Drug (Control) Ordinance 1982.[54] It was accepted immediately. High-alcohol drugs were to be destroyed within three months. Traditional manufacturers were also instructed not to use Western allopathic names and not to produce allopathic medicines under the guise of traditional medicine.

Traditionally, Ayurvedic and Unani medicines are sold through crude promotional means which take advantage of people's ignorance and fear about, for example, involuntary emission of semen (spermatorrhoea), impotency, thinness of semen and reduced vitality in men and women. Two products with an alcohol content of over 40 per cent are Mritosanjibani Sudha and Mritosanjibani Sura (two kinds of 'heavenly wine for revitalising the dead'). Manufacturers claim that Mritosanjibani also contains 27 active ingredients which are effective in treating over 80 diseases and symptoms. Mritosanjibani was banned and withdrawn before Mustafa took over the office of health secretary.

Traditional drug manufacturers were most upset with the alcohol-related recommendation. They found a champion for their cause in Professor N. A. Khan, a former professor of biochemistry and chairman of the Bangladesh Council of Scientific and Industrial Research. Once a respected person, Professor Khan was advisor to two big traditional medicine manufacturing units, Ayurvedic Pharmacy and Shakti Aushadhaloy, which were owned by the nephew of the health secretary.

Professor Khan certified that Mritosanjibani must contain 42 per cent alcohol to retain all its medicinal properties. He stated that this drug was extremely valuable for postnatal women, and for the 'hungry masses' or the 'proletariat' in general.[55] He further stated that the problem lay not with the medicines themselves but with self-prescription. Practitioners of traditional medicine also demanded that Mritosanjibani and similar products with a high alcohol content should not be banned but that the government should ensure that all drugs, including these, were sold under prescription only. Their statement was very much in line with that of the BMA.

There were many more harmful traditional medicines on the market which were not listed in any government document as traditional medicines were not under the purview of the Drugs Act of 1940. When the Director of the Drug Administration, Dr Nurul Anwar, started taking stock of traditional medicines, Ayurvedic manufacturers suddenly raised the objection that the government was interferring in the religious affairs of the Hindu community, as these drugs are manufactured according to the Hindu Shasthra (religious book). To prove their point, they managed to secure a WHO assignment for an Indian consultant on traditional medicine (possibly with the blessing of the health secretary). However, two interesting points came to light which undermined the 'sacrosanct' position of Ayurvedic medicine: first, that most owners of Ayurvedic medicine firms in Bangladesh were Muslims; and, second, that strict observance of the Shasthra required that these medicines be treated with gomutra (the urine of the sacred cow) during the manufacturing process, but that this rule was not followed anywhere in the sub-continent, including Bangladesh.

The useless medicines of Schedule III and those of the traditional medicinal systems were given another but final extension of life, to 30 June 1984. Most newspapers, including those which opposed the NDP, supported the government's action on traditional medicine. *Ittefaq* commented that Mritosanjibani was creating social problems and that immediate action must be taken to prevent its production.[56]

The final episode in the first chapter

Transnational companies do not have a particularly large market in Bangladesh but were greatly concerned that unless the NDP was nipped in the bud the Bangladesh example could affect the policies of other countries. Their fears began to come true: on 23 July 1983 the Indian Government banned the manufacture and sale of 25 drugs with immediate effect. These included amidopyrines, hydro-xyquioline, tetracycline oral liquid preparations, irrational combina-tions of multiple antibiotics and sulphanomides, antibiotics and vitamins, analgesics with vitamins and antibiotics, and steroids and analgesics.[57]

The drug bill of the National Health Service (NHS) in Britain was also hurting the British Government. Between 1974 and 1984, it rose from £250 million to £1.4 billion, an increase of 79 per cent after adjustment for inflation. Norman Fowler, the British health minister, announced in November 1984 that in seven designated therapeutic categories only certain listed products would be pre-scribed under the NHS. These categories were: analgesics for mild to moderate pain; benzodiazepines, sedatives and tranquillisers; bitters and tonics; cough and cold remedies; indigestion remedies; laxatives; and vitamins. The restriction would save £100 million.[58] In the House of Commons debate, the Bangladesh National Drug Policy was cited as an example of effective action on drugs. On 1 April 1985, 1,800 drugs were withdrawn from the list of medicines that could be prescribed under the NHS.[59]

From mid-1984 the drug companies launched a final assault on the NDP. An article in *The Pulse* claimed: '23 million dollars withdrawn from planned investments by transnationals: Drug Policy now a total failure.'[60] This is a common tactic: whenever a new government tries to change existing policy in favour of consumers, corporations all over the world issue threats about the withdrawal of investments. In 1993, the US Pharmaceutical Manufacturers Association (PMA) tried to frighten the Clinton Administration: 'Investors run like rabbits from the pharmaceutical stocks and PMA companies have lost US$150 billion in market value in the past year.'[61]

In Bangladesh, the drug industry succeeded in securing the replacement of Dr Nurul Anwar, the honest and knowledgeable director of the Drug Administration, with Dr M. Jahangir, a man who was known to be sympathetic to the industry.

The drug industry tried hard to discredit Sabar Janya Shasthaya (Health For All, HFA), and its publication of the same name which was proving quite effective in propagating the ideals of the NDP. HFA was achieving a reasonable measure of success in exposing, through newspaper features and advertisements, the wrong use of medicines and the reasons for the banning of certain medicines. It was actively supported by the Swedish Health Action International (HAI), War on Want (the British NGO), and Gonoshasthaya Kendra (GK). The new Drug Controller, in collusion with BASS, tried in vain to stop HFA's media campaign. They attempted to do so on the grounds of alleged violation of Section 14 of the Drug (Control) Ordinance 1982, which states: 'No person shall publish or take any part in the publication of any advertisements which relates to the use of any drugs or contains any claim in respect of therapies or treatment without the prior approval of the Licensing Authority.'

The drug industry was angry with Gonoshasthaya Kendra and Gonoshasthaya Pharmaceutical Ltd (GPL), as it was GPL which informed the government about the international prices of raw materials and packaging materials and which supplied information whenever the government sought it. GPL considered this to be part of its public responsibility.

On 18 August 1984, over 2,000 hired hooligans attempted to set fire to the GPL factory. While trying to fend off the attackers, 63 female and 21 male GK workers were severely wounded. The arson attempt was followed by malicious newspaper propaganda about GPL and GK, which continued over the next four months.[62] Various political parties were misled into taking sides against GPL without a full understanding of the problem. However, despite a call by *The Pulse* to review the drug policy,[63] all became quiet on the pharmaceutical front, at least until the end of 1986.

An interesting development occurred on 9 November 1986 when BASS, which had fought tooth and nail against the NDP since 1982, suddenly printed a full-page newspaper advertisement in several dailies, declaring that '... the ordinance [The Drugs (Control)

Ordinance (1982)] represents a philosophy whose scope extends beyond the need of today into [the] realms of [the] future.... It has been applied, tested and has to its credit today many examples of beneficial aspects.' In the advertisement, BASS showed by means of graphs the substantial drop in imports but dramatic growth in local production. It urged MPs to ratify the ordinance into an Act in the forthcoming winter session of the Bangladesh Parliament, 'thereby ensuring the local pharmaceutical industry and the Bangladesh people continue to benefit from revolutionary policy.'[64]

By then, Golam Mustafa, the health secretary, had left the department.

Pricing policy reviewed

In pursuance of the NDP recommendations for control of prices of finished drugs and pharmaceutical raw materials a four-person committee headed by Professor M. A. Mannan, Vice-Chancellor of Dhaka University and Professor of Pharmacy, was set up in 1987 to formulate a pricing policy. The other committee members were Salman Rahman, the managing director of Beximco Pharmaceutical and now President of both BASS and the Chamber of Commerce; Dr Humayun K. M. A. Hye; and Dr Zafrullah Chowdhury. The committee based its recommendations on a simple formula of adding 100 per cent to the unit price, inclusive of import duties, taxes, import licence fees and transportation costs of individual raw materials and packaging materials. An extra mark-up of between 50 and 225 per cent was allowed for the cost of processing, quality control, commission for distribution and retailing. The scale of mark-up was as follows (Table 4.1):

A. 50 per cent for simple repacking which does not require any processing;

B. 100 per cent for oral products other than antibiotics, creams and ointments, etc;

C. 125 per cent for oral antibiotics, coated tablets, sustained-release dosage forms, soluble tablets, suppositories and vaginal tablets;

D. 175 per cent for products requiring terminal sterilisations and hormonal preparations etc;

E. 225 per cent for products requiring total aseptic facilities.

Sales tax, value added tax (VAT), other duties and surcharges, are also added to reach the maximum retail price (MRP).

Table 4.1: Mark-up calculation for maximum retail prices in Bangladesh in 1987

Category of drugs	Cost of raw and packing material	Production/ overhead cost and profit	Distribution/ trade commission: 8 per cent on trade price	Trade/whole-sale price	Retailers' commission: 15 per cent on MRP	Maximum retail price (MRP) without excise duty/VAT
A	100	17.30	10.20	127.50	22.50	150.00
B	100	56.40	13.60	170.00	30.00	200.00
C	100	75.95	15.30	191.25	33.75	225.00
D	100	115.05	18.70	233.75	41.25	275.00
E	100	154.25	22.10	276.25	48.75	325.00

Source: Bangladesh Drug Administration, 1992.

The committee further recommended that companies with better quality control and good manufacturing practice (GMP) could have an extra mark-up of 10 per cent; and that any company which would agree to donate a certain sum for medical research at the university or the Medical Research Council could likewise have an extra 10 per cent mark-up. Unfortunately, the last two provisions were not accepted by BASS. A Pricing Subcommittee was set up to review the prices of imported raw material and packaging material charged by ten large and medium companies and five small companies. On this basis, prices are reviewed every six months and take dollar fluctuation and government changes in taxation into account as well. It is worth remembering that quality assurance and measures to ensure good manufacturing practice account for less than 5 per cent of the total cost.

In 1989, a further increase in mark-ups resulted in an increase from 100 to 125 per cent in group B, from 125 to 130 per cent in group C, from 175 to 180 per cent in group D, and from 225 to 240 per cent in group E (Table 4.2). Despite this price regime, many companies, both national and transnational, are selling below the MRP.

It was not the specific mark-up restrictions but the principle of price controls introduced by the Bangladesh Government that upset the TNCs. The drug industry's voice was later strengthened by the head of the Industry and Energy Unit of the World Bank, who wrote to the Bangladesh Government on 8 June 1992: '[The] prices of most drugs are determined by competitive market forces rather than their MRP. Flat-rate price controls hurt those firms which spend money on quality assurance and maintain good manufacturing practices.' The same World Bank letter further states: 'It is the generally held view, which we share, that a decontrol of prices would not lead to an abnormal rise in prices because of the competitive structure of the market.'[65] (See Appendix 2)

Pricing policies in other countries

The escalation of drug prices is a matter of concern for all countries. It is easy for prices to soar in countries without a price control system. In Malaysia, the prices of most drugs are 10 to 293 per cent higher than in Australia and the UK, and rose annually by 20.7 per cent when the rate of inflation was 7 per cent.[66] Drug prices in the USA, the country with the most developed free-market economy and with no price regulation whatsoever, tell a similar story. David

Table 4.2 : Amended mark-up for pricing of locally produced drugs in 1989

Category of drugs	Cost of raw and packing material	Production/ overhead cost and profit	Distribution/ trade commission: 8 per cent on trade price	Trade/whole-sale price	Retailers' commission: 15 per cent on MRP	Maximum retail price (MRP) without excise duty/VAT
A	100	17.30	10.20	127.50	22.50	150.00
B	100	75.95	15.30	191.25	33.75	225.00
C	100	79.86	15.65	195.50	34.50	230.00
D	100	118.96	19.04	238.00	42.00	280.00
E	100	165.88	23.12	289.00	51.00	340.00

Source: Bangladesh Drug Administration, 1992.

Schulke, Chief Health Policy Adviser to the Democratic representative Ron Wyden, who proposed curbing the US pharmaceutical industry's power over prices, has observed: 'It is not a free market when companies can regally glide into the market and set their prices at whatever level they like.'[67] Dee Fensterer, President of the US Generic Pharmaceutical Industry Association (GPIA), asked the US government to stop reimbursing two pharmaceutical industries for the same product at two different price levels to ensure equal competition between members of PMA and GPIA.[68]

The overpricing situation in the USA was admitted by the outgoing PMA chairman, Paul Freiman: 'Our industry has been tuned into an unrealistic wavelength for far too long. We have, instead, been working on a status quo basis, cloaking ourselves in the righteousness of our very exciting research.'[69]

As a response to the unregulated situation, the Clinton administration has been forced to consider price controls, restrictive formularies, therapeutic substitution and prior approval requirements.

Furthermore, as Canadian drug prices are one third of US prices, due to the review carried out by Canada's Patented Medicine Prices Review Board, a US Prescription Drug Price Review Board Bill was introduced in the US Senate by Representative Richard Durbin in 1993. The companies are now required to report every new drug price and price increase, and also to provide information on pricing in the USA and other countries, as well as R&D, manufacturing and marketing costs.[70] This has striking similarities with the Bangladesh pricing policy.

It is worth remembering that the high price of patented drugs led to the fast expansion of the generics market in the USA. This is expected to exceed 50 per cent of the total market by 1995 and further increase after the year 2000 when patents of over 200 drugs, worth US$22 billion in sales in 1991, will end. Senator David Pryor, Chairman of the Senate Special Committee on Aging, considers that the increasing number of mergers, as TNCs buy up generics companies, demonstrate 'control over pricing policies by brand companies'.[71]

Most governments of industrialised countries have adopted a range of methods as a cost-containment strategy:

- reduction of non-essential, high-cost and high-volume drugs from the list of reimbursable drugs – known as 'negative listing'. In 1991, Portugal withdrew 1,000 drugs out OF 5,000 marketed products. In 1994, Switzerland added 800 medicines to the negative list which already had 200 drugs, a de-listing with projected savings worth US$38 million annually;[72]

- stringent examination and negotiation (especially in France, the UK and Canada) to fix prices of new products and control price increases;
- reduction of promotional expenditure. Both France and Spain place limits on promotional spending;
- reference pricing schemes. Reimbursement is allowed up to a maximum level for a particular therapeutic class based on the price of a reference product, chosen on the basis of efficacy, tolerance, usefulness and price. The Netherlands and Denmark have a system of this kind;
- monitoring the prescription habits of physicians and promotion of generic prescription. Germany and the UK have such programmes in operation. Norwegian doctors are told to prescribe the cheapest multisource products, a list of which is published every year by the regulatory authority. French doctors are provided with a number of good medical practice guidelines, of which 17 are related to the prescribing of medicines. The health ministry of Nova Scotia province in Canada warned doctors that if any prescription was found to be inappropriate, the doctor who had issued it would be billed. This warning resulted in savings of Canadian $11 million within five months;[73]
- consumer education on drug prices and over-the-counter drugs;
- a profit-monitoring system (in existence in the UK) whereby the price of a product is freely set by the manufacturers within the framework of a negotiated profit return;
- substitution of costly brands with cheaper brands or generic versions (in Australia, New Zealand and some states of the USA).

Some Third World countries have introduced price controls. Egypt is one country where drug prices are controlled and where the health ministry has been particularly reluctant to approve registration of expensive new products.[74] In June 1993, the Government of Pakistan introduced ceilings on drug prices for various categories of medicine, binding on all companies irrespective of origin. Identical products bearing different brand names have to be sold at the same price,[75] as in Bangladesh.

Notes

1. Ahmed, S., 'WHO prescription: Only 248 basic drugs enough, 1742 unnecessary drugs to be banned', *Bangladesh Times*, Dhaka, 1 June 1982.

2. 'Commerce chief sees need for "little bribes" ', *San Francisco Chronicle*, 24 March 1981; Miller, N. C., 'US business overseas: back to bribery?', *Wall Street Journal*, 30 April 1981, quoted in Silverman, M., Lydecker, M. and Lee, P. R., *Bad Medicine*, op. cit.

3. Brightbill, Tim, 'Political Action Committees: How much influence will $7.7 million buy?, *Health Week*, Washington, 5 November 1990.

4. Ibid.

5. Declassified Document, Department of State A/CDC/MR Washington DC, 13 January, 1983.

6. 'Drug Policy Invokes Mixed Reaction', *The New Nation*, Dhaka, 10 June 1982.

7. Declassified Document, 'Memorandum of conversation – New Drug Policy', Department of State A/CDC/MR, Washington DC, 13 January 1983.

8. Ibid.

9. Ibid.

10. 'Bangladesh unleashed by US: George Bush blesses drug industry, damns regulation', *Multinational Monitor*, August 1982.

11. 'Drug Policy Invokes Mixed Reaction', *New Nation*, op. cit.

12. Personal communication with the author.

13. Government of the People's Republic of Bangladesh, Ministry of Law and Land Reforms, Law and Parliamentary Affairs Division, 'The Drugs (Control) Ordinance, 1982, No.VIII of 1982: An Ordinance to Control Manufacture, Import, Distribution and Sale of Drugs', *Bangladesh Gazette Extraordinary*, Dhaka, 12 June 1982.

14. The Drugs (Control) Ordinance 1982, op. cit.

15. Engman, Lewis A., letter to Lt. General Hossain Mohammad Ershad, Pharmaceutical Manufacturers Association, Washington DC, 16 June 1982.

16. Declassified Documents, 'Confidential Dacca - 4022', Department of State A/CDC/MR, Washington DC, 13 January 1983.

17. *The Lancet*, London, 19 June 1982.

18. US Senate, Committee on the Judiciary, Subcommittee on Anti-Trust and Monopoly, *Administered Prices in the Drug Industry 1959–62*, US Government Printing, Washington D.C., 1965. The committee was chaired by Senator Kefauver and thus became known as the Kefauver Committee.

19. Sainsbury Committee, *Report of the Committee of Enquiry into the Relationship of the Pharmaceutical Industry with the National Health Services, 1965–67*, HMSO, London, 1967.

20. Hathi Committee, *Report of the Committee on the Drugs and Pharmaceutical Industry*, Ministry of Petroleum and Chemicals, Government of India, New Delhi, April 1975.

21. Harris, Richard, *The Real Voice*, MacMillan, New York, 1964.

22. Kintanar, Q. L., 'Marketing Policy: Focus on The Philippines', in *Prescription for Change*, Philippine Center for Investigative Journalism/Dag Hammarskjöld Foundation, Sweden, 1992.

23. *The Pulse*, Dhaka, 20 June 1982.

24. *New Nation*, Dhaka, 22 August 1982.

25. 'Over 60 professors, doctors complain to BMA: Doctors demand disciplinary action', *The Pulse* (special issue), Dhaka, 9 August 1982.

26. Braithwaite, J., *Corporate Crime in the Pharmaceutical Industry*, Routledge & Kegan Paul, London, 1984.

27. Muller, M., *The Health of Nations: A North-South Investigation*, Faber and Faber, London, 1982.

28. Statement by Douglas Hurd, quoted in Chetley, A., *Bangladesh: Finding the Right Prescription*, War on Want, London, 1982.

29. Declassified Documents, 'Bangladesh 6/24 meeting', Department of State A/CD/MR, Washington DC, 13 January 1983.

30. Ibid.

31. Letters from US Senators and the State Department, quoted in Kintanar, Q. L., 'Marketing Policy: Focus on The Philippines', in *Prescription for Change*, op. cit.

32. 'Crisis in the Drug Industry: A Practical Study of the Conspiracy to Destroy the Drug Industry', BASS advertisement, *Ittefaq*, 14 August 1982.

33. 'Crisis in Drug Industry: Conspiracy against the nation's drug industry must be thwarted – A realistic study by Bangladesh Ausadh Shilpa Shamity', *New Nation*, 22 August 1982.

34. Bennett, Jonathan, 'Bangladesh: taking on the drug companies', *Guardian*, London, 25 August 1982.

35. WHO, World Health Assembly Documents, A35/A/SR/5, World Health Organization, Geneva, May 1982.

36. Wolfe, Sidney M. and Gordon, Benjamin, letter to Major General Shamsul Huq, Minister of Health and Population Control, Dacca, Public Citizen Health Research Group, Washington DC, 9 August 1982.

37. Ibid.

38. Ibid.

39. Wolfe, Sidney M., Bergman, Eve, Gordon, Ben, Public Citizen Health Research Group, letter to Honourable George P. Shultz, Secretary of State, Washington DC, 18 August 1982.

40. Ibid.

41. Ibid.

42. Chorlton, Penny, 'US is aiding drug companies in Bangladesh', *Washington Post*, Washington DC, 19 August 1982.

43. Ibid.

44. Declassified Document, 'NEA Press Guidance – Bangladesh Government Drug Policy', 19 August 1982, Department of State A/CDC/MR, Washington DC, 13 January 1983.

45. Declassified Document, 'Memorandum from EB/IFD/OIA Philip T. Lincoln, Jr. to EB/IFD-MS. Constable', 31 August 1982, Department of State A/CDC/MR, Washington DC, 13 January 1983.

46. Moore, Powell A., Assistant Secretary for Congressional Relations, letter to Honourable Charles McC. Mathias, Jr., United States Senate, Washington DC, 8 September 1983.

47. Kirby, Harmon E., Deputy Assistant Secretary (Acting), Department of State, letter to Sidney M. Wolfe, Director, Public Citizen Health Research Group, Washington DC, 31 August 1982.

48. Wolfe, Sidney M. and Gordon, Benjamin, Public Citizen Health Research Group, letter to Harman E. Kirby, Deputy Assistant Secretary (Acting), Department of State, Washington DC, 15 September 1982.

49. Sawatsky, J. and Cashore, H., 'Inside dope', *This Magazine*, Vol. 20, No. 3, 1986, pp. 4–12, quoted in Lexchin, Joel, *Pharmaceuticals, Patents and Policies: Canada and Bill C–22*, The Canadian Centre for Policy Alternatives, Ottawa, February 1992.

50. Pavit, Laurie, letter to Major General Shamsul Huq, Minister of Health and Population Control, quoted in 'Drug Policy hailed', *Bangladesh Times*, Dacca, 5 August 1982.

51. Veitch, A., 'The Great Drugs Raid', *Guardian*, London, 13 July 1982.

52. 'Medicine Exports: Drugs on the Run', *The Economist*, London, 11 September 1982.

53. 'Government urged to stick to new drug policy: joint statement by 229 renowned intellectuals, physicians and journalists', *Bangladesh Times*, 5 August 1982.

54. The Drugs (Control) Ordinance 1982, op. cit.

55. Ahmed, Shehab, 'Alcohol Business in the Name of Herbal Medicines', *Weekly Bichitra*, Dhaka, 28 October 1983.

56. Editorial, *Ittefaq*, Dhaka, 23 October 1983.

57. *Notification of Banned Drugs*, GSR 578(E), Ministry of Health and Family Welfare, Government of India, New Delhi, 23 July 1983.

58. Bateman, D. N., 'The Selected List', *British Medical Journal*, London, 1 May 1993.

59. Communication from Department of Health and Social Security, UK, quoted in Tiranti, D. J., *Essential Drugs: The Bangladesh Example – Four Years On*, IOCU/New Internationalist, War on Want, London, 1986.

60. *The Pulse*, Dhaka, 16 April 1984.

61. 'PMA Chairman warns of more rebates', *Scrip*, London, 9 April 1993.

62. News on GPL and GK in various Bangladesh daily and weekly newspapers published between August 1984 and January 1985.

63. 'A readjusted policy can be a good revenue earner: It's time to review the Drug Policy', *The Pulse*, Dhaka, 6 January 1986.

64. BASS advertisement, 'Appeal to Members of Parliament', various newspapers of Dhaka, 9 November 1986.

65. Hasan, Abid, letter to Ayub Quadri, Joint Secretary, Economic Relations Division, Government of Bangladesh, Dhaka, 8 June 1992.

66. Kaur, N., 'Curb soaring prices of pharmaceuticals', *Utusan Konsummer*, Consumer Association of Penang, mid-December 1994.

67. Tobias, Greg, 'More pressure on Free Pricing in the US', *Scrip Magazine*, London, April 1992.

68. 'Task force grilling for US industry', *Scrip*, London, 6 April 1993.

69. 'PMA Chairman warns of more rebates', *Scrip*, London, 9 April 1993, op. cit.

70. 'US Pricing Board Bill introduced', *Scrip*, London, 9 April 1993.

71. 'Prior warning on anti-competitive activities', *Scrip*, London, 17 August 1993.

72. '800 products deleted in Switzerland', *Scrip*, London, 13 September, 1994.

73. 'Script warning to Canadian GPs saves Can. $11 million', *Scrip*, London, 29 July 1994.

74. 'PHRMA barriers to trade in Egypt', *Scrip*, London, December 1994.

75. 'Deregulating Drug Prices', editorial in *The Dawn*, Karachi, 23 June 1993.

5

Achievements and limitations

Substantial benefits have derived from Bangladesh's National Drug Policy (NDP). The gains are evident when prices, production figures and quality indicators at the time the policy was introduced are compared with those of a decade later (1992):

- Essential drugs increased from 30 per cent to 80 per cent of local production.
- Drug prices stabilised, increasing by only 20 per cent, compared with an increase of 178.8 per cent in the consumer price index. The drop in price in real terms made drugs more affordable.
- Bangladesh companies increased their share of local production from 35 per cent to over 60 per cent – overall, local production increased by 217 per cent.
- Less dependence on imports and prioritisation of useful products saved the country approximately US$600 million.
- The quality of products improved – the proportion of drugs found to be substandard fell from 36 per cent to 9 per cent.[1]

Increased local drug production and lower prices

It is evident that the availability of essential drugs has increased remarkably with the increase in local production, the value of which grew from Taka 1,730 million in 1981 to Taka 5,500 million in 1991 (Table 5.1). During this period, however, the value of the Taka against the US dollar fell sharply. In 1981, the conversion rate was Taka 16.26 to US$1; in 1991, it was Taka 35.2 to US$1. By 1993, it had fallen to Taka 39.13 to US$1.[2]

Pending the final compilation of production information from all companies, the director of the Drug Administration estimated that total drug production in 1994 would be around Taka 10,000 million. In 1993, the figure was Taka 8,900 million.[3]

Table 5.1: Increase in local production of drugs in Bangladesh during 1981–91 in million Taka and nominal prices; decrease in imports of finished drugs in million US$

Year	Total local production (Taka mn.)	Production by local national companies (Taka mn.)	Imports of finished drugs		Official conversion rate of US$ 1 to Taka
			(US$ mn.)	(Taka mn.)	
1981	1,730	613	17.5	284	16.26
1982	2,160	842	13.5	270	20.07
1983	2,260	1160	9.7	232	23.80
1984	2,830	1470	12.1	301	24.94
1985	3,283	1864	13.0	337	25.96
1986	3,500	2080	16.1	482	29.89
1987	4,048	2315	10.1	310	30.63
1988	4,383	2944	8.4	263	31.25
1989	5,000	3008	7.6	244	32.25
1990	5,300	3429	8.9	294	32.89
1991	5,500	3375	8.9	315	35.25

Source: Bangladesh Drug Administration, 1992.

Increased local production led to a decrease in imported drugs, which are now mostly items on the supplementary list. Eighty per cent of locally produced drugs are for primary and secondary health care. Pursuance of NDP objectives to procure raw materials at the most competitive prices led to a sharp decrease in the prices of raw materials (Table 5.2) and in turn to a fall in the maximum retail price (MRP) of finished drugs.

The pricing system for finished drugs recommended by the Mannan Committee (1987) discouraged superfluous or luxury packaging. Accordingly, the Drug Administration does not include costs of unnecessary packaging materials when calculating the cost of finished drugs. The effect is clearly reflected in the decrease in imported packaging materials and the increase in imported raw materials (Table 5.3). Strict adherence to this principle would further ensure cheaper drugs and prevent the promotion of poor-quality drugs in fancy dress. Imported packaging material fell from 42 per cent of the value of imported raw material in 1981 to 13.4 per cent in 1991.

The retail prices of most of the drugs produced locally showed a downward trend between 1981 and 1991/2, or at worst were static (Table 5.4). The prices of a small number of drugs including aspirin, paracetamol, ampicillin, amoxycillin, cloxacillin, antacids and chloroquine, went up. The first four of these are manufactured from locally

Table 5.2:   Reduction in prices of raw materials 1981-91

Raw material	Prices in US$/kg		Reduction in percentage
	1981	1991	
Amoxycillin trihydrate (local)	130	3,225*	29.6
Ampicillin trihydrate (local)	120	2,870*	32.1
Cloxacillin	95	70	26.3
Doxycycline	1,500	78	94.8
Fursemide	703	70	90.0
Glibenclamide	2,350	180	92.3
Hyoscine Butylbromide	1,358	390	71.3
Ibuprofen	32	16	50.0
Levamisole	128	31	75.8
Mebendazole	287	19	93.4
Metaclopramide	200	105	47.5
Metronidazole	56	17	69.6
Oxytetracycline	54	16	70.4
Propranolol	490	25	94.9
Rifampicin	473	178	62.4
Sulphamethoxazole	37	14	62.2
Tetracycline HCl	64	24	62.5
Trimethprim	60	33	45.0

* Raw materials produced locally and sold in Taka currency. The conversion rate in 1991 was 35.25 Taka to 1 US$. The price in US$ would then be 91 and 81 respectively.

Source: Bangladesh Drug Administration, 1992.

Table 5.3:   Pharmaceutical sector imports 1981–91 in US$ million and nominal prices; equivalent amount in million Taka given for information

Year	Imports of raw materials		Imports of packaging materials		Official conversion rate of US$1 to Taka
	(US$ mn.)	(Taka mn.)	(US$ mn.)	(Taka mn.)	
1981	25.1	407	10.5	171	16.26
1982	24.3	487	6.6	132	20.07
1983	28.4	676	6.9	165	23.80
1984	38.2	952	9.2	230	24.94
1985	37.8	982	9.4	245	25.96
1990	45.1	1,483	6.6	217	32.89
1991	56.1	1,978	7.5	265	35.25

Source: Bangladesh Drug Administration, 1992

Table 5.4: Changes in nominal retail prices of 30 important drugs in Taka and, for comparison, US$ in the period 1981 – 1991/92

Product	Retail price in Taka			Retail price in US$		
	1981	1991/92	change (%)	1981	1991/92	change (%)
Amitriptyline tablet 25 mg	0.80	0.45	−43.7	0.05	0.01	−74.1
Amoxycillin capsule 250 mg	2.50	2.90	16.0	0.15	0.08	−46.6
Ampicillin capsule 250 mg	1.70	2.50	47.1	0.10	0.07	−30.0
Ampicillin syrup 60 ml	21.00	33.00*	57.1	1.29	0.94	−27.1
Antacid tablet	0.30	0.50	66.7	0.02	0.01	−23.1
Aspirin tablet 300 mg	0.10	0.44	340.0	0.01	0.01	103.0
Atenolol tablet 100 mg	6.00	3.30	−45.0	0.37	0.09	−74.6
Chlorrhexidine sol. 112 ml	10.53	16.68	58.4	0.65	0.47	−26.9
Chloroquine tablet 250 mg	0.39	1.00	156.4	0.02	0.03	18.3
Cimetidine tablet 200 mg coated	2.00ᵃ	1.45	−27.5	0.08	0.04	−51.0
Cloxacillin capsule 500 mg	3.60ᵇ	5.65	56.9	0.14	0.16	11.0
Cotrimoxazole tablet	2.00	0.65	−67.5	0.12	0.02	−85.0
Buprofen tablet 10 mg	1.36	0.83	−39.0	0.08	0.02	−71.8
Dapsone tablet 100 mg	0.20	0.16	−20.0	0.01	0.00	−63.1
Diazepam tablet 5 mg	0.30	0.20	−33.3	0.02	0.01	−69.2
Fluocinolone cream 5 mg	12.00	26.00	116.7	0.74	0.74	−0.1
Fursemide tablet 40 mg	0.60	0.50	−16.7	0.04	0.01	−61.6
Indomethacin capsule 25 mg	1.91	0.52	−72.8	0.12	0.01	−87.4
Levamisole syrup 30 ml	13.00	9.35	−28.1	0.80	0.27	−66.8
Levamisole tablet 40 mg	1.30	0.41	−68.5	0.08	0.01	−85.5
Mebendazole tablet 100 mg	2.11	0.70	−66.8	0.13	0.02	−84.7
Metronidazole tablet 200 mg	0.70	0.63	−10.0	0.04	0.02	−58.5
Metronidazole I.V. 500 mg/100 ml	248.75	55.00	−77.9	15.30	1.56	−89.8
Nifedipine capsule 10 mg	4.60	0.32	−428.0	0.28	0.01	−96.8
Oxytetracycline capsule 250 mg	1.05	1.00	−4.8	0.06	0.03	−56.1
Paracetamol tablet 500 mg	0.25	0.52	−108.0	0.02	0.02	14.4
Propranolol tablet 40 mg	1.00	0.32	−68.0	0.06	0.01	−85.2
Ranitidine tablet 150 mg	3.00ᶜ	2.05	−31.7	0.12	0.06	−49.7
Rifampicin capsule 150 mg	5.18	3.50	−32.4	0.32	0.10	−68.8
Vitamin B complex tablet	0.74	0.42	−43.2	0.05	0.01	−73.8

a) 1983 price, b) 1984 price, c) 1985 price, *for 100 ml bottle

Source: Bangladesh Drug Administration, 1992.

produced raw materials. An increased mark-up for oral antibiotics from 125 to 130 per cent over the price of raw and packaging materials and additional value added tax (VAT) on all locally produced raw and packaging materials were also partly responsible for the increased price. If the retail prices of amoxycillin, ampicillin, antacid and paracetamol were calculated in US dollars these products would also show a 46.6 per cent, 30 per cent, 23.1 per cent and 14.4 per cent decrease respectively.

Table 5.4 shows retail prices in Taka and, for easy reference, in US dollars. The downward trend of prices is more dramatic in US dollars: the minimum price decrease was 23.1 per cent while the maximum decrease was 96.8 per cent. The highest price increase occurred in the case of aspirin, which went up from Taka 0.10 to Taka 0.44.

These prices are inclusive of 15 per cent VAT, which was not in existence in 1982. Customs duties on pharmaceutical raw materials were 10 per cent or less in 1981, but over the next decade varied between 10 and 25 per cent.

The abolition of transfer pricing

Drug manufacturers' total profits have gone up, because of the increased volume of production, while the unit profit has gone down, to the benefit of consumers. TNCs can no longer dream of the easy profits they were making before the introduction of the NDP, when profit levels were much higher than those suggested by declared turnover and profit figures. The National Drug Policy effectively brought to an end transfer pricing and over-invoicing for imports of capital machinery, raw materials and packaging materials, which were common practices before its introduction in 1982.

When establishing factories in Third World countries, TNCs have made no provision for controlling pollution or tackling other environmental problems. Their preoccupation has always been to instal the factory with the least investment possible and to recover the total investment in as short a time as possible. Political instability in Third World countries has often been used as a good excuse for this behaviour. In fact, TNCs' investments in the Third World through finance capital are negligible, as is evident in the case of Bangladesh; actual cash capital investment is even less. Through their high volume of sales in relation to their paltry investments, TNCs in Bangladesh make enough profit to recover their whole investment within two to three years of beginning operations. It is worth

emphasising that the investments of TNCs are not for the manufacture of drugs from raw materials but for establishing repackaging
warehouses in the Third World.[4]

Good dividends from small changes

Before the implementation of the NDP, most liquid products except
antibiotics used to be marketed in 100 ml or larger bottles, while
antibiotic suspensions and dry syrups were marketed in 60 ml bottles,
which is grossly inadequate as most antibiotics are prescribed four
times a day for a minimum period of five days. With the NDP, the
dispensing of antibiotic dry syrups and other chemotherapy liquids
in 100 ml bottles was made mandatory. This not only makes sense
scientifically, but is also cheaper, comparatively, than buying the
drug in 60 ml bottles.

Criterion 14 of the NDP debars TNCs from producing antacids
and oral vitamins. Although this meant the loss of a big share of the
market, it forced them to compete for market shares in other
products such as antibiotics.

Almost all TNCs now produce the same antibiotics, and other
effective drugs are competing with each other. Eight TNCs now
manufacture ampicillin and amoxycillin. TNCs in Bangladesh can no
longer practise a monopoly cartel system. Moreover, the NDP is
applied equally in both the public and the private sector, still one of
the major sore points for drug companies. However, TNCs continue
to mislead other Third World countries with the propaganda that
essential drugs are only for the public sector, not for the private sector.

Circumventing the generics issue

Many countries have attempted to introduce generic names, or to
substitute cheaper generic drugs for brand-name drugs. Since brand
names ensure that a company continues to benefit from a patent
even after its expiry, it is not surprising that drug companies every-
where, whether in the USA, Canada or the UK, Chile, India or
Pakistan, have fought hard with the help of the medical establishment to prevent the introduction of a 'generics-only' policy and
have often won.

Initially, in Bangladesh, the Expert Committee proposed that 45
drugs for use in primary health care be manufactured and sold only
under generic names. But the committee was well aware of the
records of failure in other countries and decided not to go for a

head-on collision on the generics issue but to devise a strategy to achieve the main benefits of generic drugs without making the marketing of drugs under generic names compulsory. It therefore made it clear that manufacturers were free to market their drugs under brand names, providing the generic name was printed underneath the brand name in the same size of type. Furthermore, it recommended that drugs with the same active ingredients be sold at the same price, irrespective of whether they were brand-name drugs, branded generics or commodity generics. With this alternative strategy, Bangladesh avoided the generics tussle but achieved the goal of making quality drugs plentifully available at a cheaper price.

A few years after Bangladesh introduced its National Drug Policy, the Philippines attempted to take radical action on drug prices through the introduction of a generics policy. Dr Alfredo Bengzon, the Philippines health minister, successfully introduced the Generic Act of 1988. This was passed unanimously in the Congress and given the blessing of President Corazon Aquino. But immediately afterwards, the Philippines Medical Association and a number of TNCs took the government to court.

This happened despite the fact that the government had for almost two years consulted widely and fully during the process of developing the Philippines National Drug Policy (PNDP). Ninety-nine individuals representing 61 different organisations participated in a series of meetings.[5] Twenty-five position papers were discussed at two national seminars, and innumerable small consultations were conducted. The framework of the PNDP was defined and drafted by 54 international experts from the World Bank, the UN and the European Community. The medical profession was involved at every stage. But when the Generic Law of 1988 was passed, members of the Philippines Medical Association, who at that time enjoyed absolute power and all the perks associated with the use of prescription drugs, came out openly against the new law.[6]

The government won the case in the Supreme Court but it lost the battle. Drug prices did not come down, in the absence of a clear-cut pricing policy and of controls over the advertising of drugs on television and radio and in the print media. In television commercials, the generic name of a drug would be displayed for the briefest of moments, while the brand name was announced repeatedly – the same technique that medical representatives use with doctors. No wonder, then, that there has so far been little net impact on the Philippine pharmaceuticals market since the Generic Act was signed into effect.[7]

Improved testing and better-quality locally produced drugs

The quality of locally manufactured drugs has improved significantly since the introduction of the NDP because of greater vigilance and because testing procedures are easier now that most products contain only one active ingredient. Large and medium-sized companies furnished their quality assurance laboratories with a reasonable amount of modern equipment and brought in qualified personnel. In 1981, only 327 products had been tested, of which 36 per cent were found to be substandard, while in 1992, 2,617 samples were examined, of which 174 were found to be of substandard quality (Table 5.5).

Table 5.5: Results of drug samples tested by drug-testing laboratories in 1981–92

Year	Total samples tested	Number of substandard drugs	Percentage of substandard drugs
1981	327	118	36.0
1985	1,187	169	14.6
1989	2,367	238	10.0
1990	3,555	298	8.4
1991	2,331	219	9.4
1992	2,617	174	6.6

Source: Bangladesh Drug Administration, 1993.

All the samples were tested in two government-run drug-testing laboratories, one in Dhaka and the other in the port city of Chittagong. Located in these two cities are 142 pharmaceutical production units (over 70 per cent of the country's total), while the remaining 57 companies are spread out in 23 small district towns. Square Pharmaceutical, located in the small town of Pabna, has the largest volume of sales. The top 15 companies, including Gonoshasthaya Pharmaceutical Ltd (GPL), control 88.7 per cent of the drugs market and are located in Dhaka, Chittagong, Pabna and Barisal. Thirty medium-sized pharmaceutical units have over 6 per cent of the market share, while the remaining 5 per cent is shared by 154 small units.

Persistence of some substandard drugs

Substandard drugs are produced mainly by the small units and some by medium-sized enterprises. An independent study, conducted in 1992 by Professor Jiben Roy and colleagues at the Pharmacy Department of Jahangirnagar University,[8] provides significant information on the quality of drugs in Bangladesh: 137 samples from 13 of the 15 top companies and 57 medium-sized and small companies were purchased from retail drug stores and examined. (Of the two other top transnational companies, Squibb was not in operation, following its merger with Bristol Myers, and Organon, a Dutch TNC, does not produce any of the eight products tested.)

The drugs tested, in various dosage forms, were paracetamol, antacid, ampicillin and vitamin B complex – among the most commonly used drugs in Bangladesh. These drugs are manufactured by most large and medium-sized companies and also by a large number of small companies (Table 5.6). Large and medium-sized companies usually produce the same drug in tablet or capsule form and as a syrup or suspension. A few also produce an injectable form. Some companies are so small that they do not have tablet facilities, and produce mainly capsules, syrups and suspensions.

Active ingredients in 37 brands were found to be far less than the required amount. The 37 substandard drugs were produced by 24 small companies, six of which had manufactured more than one substandard product. Out of the 24 companies, 21 had marketed substandard drugs during the period July 1988–June 1991, as was evident from the self-withdrawal advertisements in the three major national dailies (Table 5.7).

A further study was undertaken of the 16 substandard brands of paracetamol tablets. This was conducted jointly by the Pharmacy Department of Jahangirnagar University and the Institute of Public Health.[9] Spectraphotometric and high pressure liquid chromatography tests provided information on the quantity of active

Table 5.6: Number of producers of various dosage forms of four common drugs

Product	Tablet	Capsule	Syrup	Suspension	Injection
Paracetamol	103	-	126	5	-
Antacid	79	-	-	132	-
Ampicillin	-	63	45*	-	8
Vitamin B complex	33	49	14	-	6

* dry syrup

Source: Bangladesh Drug Administration, 1993.

Table 5.7: Number of substandard drugs in an independent study of locally produced drugs in Bangladesh

Products	Number of brands tested	Substandard drugs (numbers)	(percentage)
Paracetamol tablet	53	16 (11)*	30.2
Ampicillin Capsule	25	10 (8)*	40.0
Cotrimexazole tablet	13	3	23.1
Cotrimexazole suspension	8	2 (2)*	25.0
Vitamin B Complex tablet	9	3	33.3
B Complex Capsule	15	1	6.7
B Complex Injection	6	1	16.7
Vitamin B-2	8	1	12.5
Total	137	37	

*The number in parenthesis denote the number of companies which had produced substandard drugs in the same category in the previous years.

Source: Roy, Jiben, 'Quality of Marketed Drugs in Developing Countries: Bangladesh - A Case Study', (Mimeo).

ingredients in the samples. Normally a paracetamol tablet must contain 500 mg of the active ingredient, plus or minus 5 per cent, but in the samples tested, the content of active paracetamol varied between 35.9 mg and 465.5 mg.

Out of the 16 substandard paracetamol producers, eleven were old culprits which had been reprimanded in the past for marketing tablets with a very low active-ingredient content. One small pharmaceutical unit, Medicare, is persistent in manufacturing substandard drugs. In 1986, it was found to be marketing a 250 mg ampicillin capsule with only 50 mg of ampicillin trihydrate.[10] Previously it had produced 15 other substandard drugs. In 1992, Medicare's 250 mg ampicillin capsule contained 146 mg of the active ingredient; one brand had 6.6 mg of ampicillin trihydrate, and another was marketing an ampicillin capsule containing no active ingredient at all.[11]

Fortunately, all the companies producing substandard drugs, if taken together, occupy only about 1 per cent of the market. These products are sold in remote rural areas at about half the price of the standard products. They are not prescribed by qualified doctors. Village practitioners are aware of the substandard antibiotics and that is why in most cases they prescribe a well-known quality brand of metronidazole, an anti-infective drug, at the same time.[12]

It is most unfortunate that the Drug Administration has never seriously tried to apply the law and punish the offenders although Article 17 of the Drug (Control) Ordinance 1982 clearly specifies that whoever manufactures or sells any substandard drug shall be punishable with imprisonment of up to five years or a fine of up to one lac (Taka 100,000) or both.[13] It seems quite likely that some officials in the Drug Administration supplement their low salaries by accepting bribes from manufacturers of substandard drugs.

The case of Flamodel paracetamol syrup

Substandard drugs or raw materials are by definition produced by registered manufacturers while counterfeit or spurious drugs are manufactured and marketed by unregistered producers. But adulterated or contaminated drugs may be produced by both authorised and unauthorised manufacturers. Unlike in most Third World countries, few spurious or adulterated drugs are marketed in Bangladesh.

A lethal paracetamol syrup manufactured with an adulterated solvent made headlines in all the newspapers in November 1992, and features have continued to be published in weeklies and other periodicals since then. The events leading up to the media coverage began two years earlier when 30 children admitted to Dhaka Shishu (Children's) Hospital died of acute renal failure, although they had no previous history of kidney infections. A young paediatrician, Dr Mohammed Hanif, suspected intake of adulterated paracetamol syrup to be the cause of death, after reading a *Newsweek* article on a similar incident in Nigeria where the death toll had diminished once use of a particular paracetamol syrup was stopped.

The brand of paracetamol syrup used by the hospital was Flamodel, manufactured by a small local pharmaceutical company, Adflame Pharmaceuticals, located just outside Dhaka and owned by a well-known general practitioner couple, Drs Anwar and Helena Pasha.

Major General Anis Waiz, a consultant physician of the Bangladesh army and a member of the Drug Control Committee of the Drug Administration for many years, was the chairman of Dhaka Children's Hospital, and retired Brigadier Maksul Hossain Chowdhury was its medical director. The hospital had no formulary and followed no system of inviting tenders from reputable drug manufacturers with quality assurance facilities and good manufacturing practice (GMP). Instead, the hospital authorities preferred to purchase direct from companies of their personal liking.

In July 1991, a member of the hospital staff telephoned the Drug Administration to report that deaths from acute renal failure had again risen sharply, coinciding with the renewed use of Flamodel. A sample of the drug was collected from the hospital for inspection, as were samples of Flamodel from Adflame Pharmaceuticals, together with the excipients used by the factory. The drug inspector suspected that instead of propylene glycol, which is normally used as a solubilising agent and diluent for paracetamol, the excipient used in the manufacture of the Flamodel samples might turn out to be diethylene glycol, a substance used in lacquer, tanning creams, various cosmetics, and as an antifreeze, lubricant, softening agent and plasticiser.[14] Diethylene glycol is about 30 per cent cheaper than propylene glycol and is imported by a range of commercial importers in Bangladesh while propylene glycol is imported exclusively by drug manufacturers with the authorisation of the Drug Administration. It is difficult to import propylene glycol in small quantities, so small companies buy it from wholesalers, the wholesale market being boosted of course by goods pilfered from large and medium-size companies and by the sale of excess imports.

However, the government drug-testing laboratory found both the paracetamol and the excipient to be of an acceptable quality and no diethylene glycol was found in the factory.

On 15 November 1992, Dr Hanif held a seminar on the subject – but without naming the company – which led to a stream of media coverage of the use of diethylene glycol in paracetamol syrup. Yet despite repeated questions by journalists and by the Drug Administrator, the hospital continued to withhold the name of the supplier. (It had made no complaint in writing at the time of the telephone complaint and did not mention that it suspected adulteration of paracetamol syrup with diethylene glycol.)

The Drug Inspector collected a sample from the medical store of Dhaka Children's Hospital, and a number of samples from the same batch from the city sales office of Adflame Pharmaceuticals. The Drug Administration also collected samples from two other companies and asked WHO to analyse them for diethylene glycol abroad. WHO sent these samples to Bangkok for testing. No diethylene glycol was detected in the sample from Adflame, while the test was positive for the sample from Bangladesh Chemical Industries (BCI) and false positive for the sample from Pacific Pharmaceuticals.

The director of the Drug Administration held a meeting with representatives from the Bangladesh Medical Association (BMA), the Pharmaceutical Society and Dr Hanif who finally, after much persuasion, disclosed the name of Adflame Pharmaceuticals but refused to give it in writing. However, he handed over another sample of Flamodel manufactured in 1990 which on analysis *was* found to contain diethylene glycol. The director of the Drug Administration immediately banned the product. On 5 December 1992, he also imposed a temporary ban on all brands of paracetamol syrup. Of 113 brands of paracetamol syrup collected from various parts of the country and tested under the direct supervision of a WHO consultant, Dr S. K. Roy, five were found to contain diethylene glycol: Flamodel, manufactured by Adflame Pharmaceuticals; Paraceton, by BCI; Paracetamol, by Polychem Industries; Prondol, by Rex Pharma; and Panacit, by City Pharmaceuticals and Chemical Works. (Samples of paracetamol from Adflame and BCI had been analysed previously by Jahangirnagar jointly with the Institute of Public Health and were found to contain 32.8 per cent and 16.8 per cent respectively of the declared content of paracetamol.)[15] Nine samples of solvents from suspected companies and from wholesalers were also collected and tested but no diethylene glycol was detected.

By 31 December 1992, the manufacturing licences of all five companies had been revoked and the companies were asked to withdraw all their paracetamol syrup. Through television, radio and newspaper advertisements the government urged the public not to use the adulterated brands.

One of the five companies, City Pharmaceuticals and Chemical Works contested the ban, claiming that the Panacit sample tested had not been manufactured by the company. The sample in question had been provided by Dhaka Children's Hospital, together with a cash receipt from a small retailer named Sutapa Pharmacy. The cash receipt contained the names of three brands of paracetamol syrup including Panacit and its batch number. Under questioning by the Drug Inspector and later by police, the shop owner persistently claimed that he did not remember from which wholesaler he had purchased the drugs. On 10 March 1993, the case against City Pharmaceuticals and Chemical Works was dropped, while cases against the other four companies were instituted in the drug court under the Drug (Control) Ordinance 1982.

On 26 April 1993, the director of the Drug Administration was served with a summons in the High Court for alleged irregularity related to the withdrawal of the ban on City Pharmaceuticals and Chemical Works. The case is still pending.

Bangladesh is not the first country to experience a tragedy with diethylene glycol. In the USA in the 1930s, 105 children ingested sulphanilamide-diethylene glycol which caused renal damage and death.[16] In Austria, in 1985, health authorities in Vienna discovered that some 50 wine producers were adulterating wine with diethylene glycol, which was resulting in instances of kidney failure and death. The wine producers were jailed and fined for their involvement in the fraud.[17]

Between 15 January and 7 February 1986, 14 patients at Sir Jamshedjee Jejeebhoy Hospital in Bombay died from the use of glycerine contaminated with diethylene glycol.[18] Justice B. Lentin, appointed to investigate the incident, held public hearings lasting over 300 days, at the end of which he found a number of the senior hospital medical staff, including the dean, Dr R. S. Chandrikapur, and the hospital superintendent, Dr V. G. Desmukh, guilty of negligence. He also found that Professor R. D. Kulkarni, a professor of pharmacology, was involved in awarding the supply contract for glycerine to a firm which, instead of producing pure glycerine, manufactured an industrial grade of the product, containing a high proportion of diethylene glycol.

Justice Lentin detailed the corrupt practices of members of the hospital's purchase committee and the collusion of the health minister, Bhai Sawant, whom he rebuked for 'misuse of power and authority'. He recommended removal of all the officials concerned, including the minister. Interestingly, both the Indian Medical Association and Maharashtra State Medical Association 'elected to maintain a discreet but embarrassed silence'.[19]

Negligence by Pfizer

There have been a small number of incidences of substandard drug production by large companies.

A glaring example of complete disregard for good manufacturing practice (GMP) was the manufacturing and marketing by Pfizer (Bangladesh) of the short-acting penicillin-G-procaine injectable as long-acting penicillin-G-benzathine (brand name Diamine Penicillin). Six consecutive batches, totalling 1.2 million units, were marketed under the wrong product name.

Pfizer ordered a supply of penicillin-G-benzathine (in its bulk form) in 1987 from Rhone Poulenc (now known as Rhone Poulenc Rorer, following its merger with the US company Rorer in 1990). Soon after the clearance of the consignment, Rhone Poulenc informed Pfizer through an urgent telex, followed by a letter, that the containers had been mislabelled and in fact contained penicillin-G-procaine. A whole year after receiving this information, Pfizer was still manufacturing and marketing phials of the drug as Diamine Penicillin.

Penicillin-G-benzathine, which is used for treating gonorrhoea, syphilis and yaws, and also for the prophylaxis of rheumatic fever, has a duration of action of three to four weeks, while penicillin-G-procaine lasts only 24 hours.

This incident proves that Pfizer's quality assurance (QA) department was neither observing GMP nor consistently testing ingredients, during the period of quarantine after a shipment's arrival, to confirm that contents tallied with the declared labels. GMP requires that all products, and none more importantly than injectables, are checked and cleared by the QA department at every stage of the operation. To err is human, but to continue an error through the production of six consecutive batches over a long period of time amounts to gross or deliberate negligence. Diamine Penicillin was de-registered for two years and Pfizer was asked to place a front-page withdrawal notice in the three major dailies, with two insertions in each (the normal requirement in such cases being one insertion in each).[20] The quality control manager lost his job and his pharmacy registration was cancelled for two years.

Spurious drugs: a logical consequence of unregulated profits

The National Drug Policy, with its organised price structure, has ensured that the incidence of counterfeiting is low in Bangladesh. It is usually high-priced drugs, whether imported or locally produced, that are subject to counterfeiting, but in Bangladesh the low price of most locally produced drugs tends to militate against the practice. No case of counterfeiting of locally produced antibiotic injectables had been reported by 1994. In Bangladesh, the injectable market is mainly confined to hospitals and private clinics, which usually buy locally produced injectables directly from the manufacturer at a reasonably low price.

However, misbranded and spurious drugs are occasionally reported in the newspapers.[21] There have been several instances of counterfeiting of four injectables: Organon's Decadurobolin (nandrolone decanoate), Roche's Rocephin (ceftriaxone), Ciba-Geigy's Volteran (diclofenac), and hydrocortisone (imported from several sources). These imported drugs are sold at much higher prices than the government-fixed MRP, which creates a real incentive for counterfeit production.

Locally produced diclofenac injectable was priced at Taka 14.71 for 75 mg in 1992, while the injectable Volteran cost Taka 50 for the same quantity. Though Ciba-Geigy has a factory in Bangladesh, it does not manufacture diclofenac locally because it can make a higher profit by importing Volteran. Greed on the part of one TNC encourages greed and deceit in others, causing the price of injectables to spiral upwards. This is what the market economy is about.

Obviously, though, there is sometimes a price to pay for greed. So long as expensive brands are permitted, and unethical and deceitful promotion of such brands continues, there is a danger of more spurious drugs penetrating the market.[22]

A number of spurious drugs banned under the NDP continue to be prescribed by unqualified village practitioners. Examples are Cibazol (sulphanilamide), Enterovioform/Mexaform (clioquinol), Novalgin (dipyrone), sulphadiazine, M&B 693 (sulphaguanadine), Sodamint (sodium bicarbonate), and Iodex (iodine ointment). The practitioners are not registered, and government documents refer to them as quacks, but often they are the only health providers in rural areas. Their lack of access to recent information on drugs encourages them to continue with these brands, which therefore remain popular in rural areas. The products are mostly smuggled into the country from India, though some are produced locally through illegal means.

The wider availability of advanced printing technology at a cheaper price has made exact copying of labels easy. Occasionally, disgruntled former employees of a large company have been involved with other profiteers in replacing the label on a cheaper injectable by one from a costlier product.

The quality of locally produced raw materials

It is usually the responsibility of manufacturing companies to identify and verify the quality of every consignment of imported or locally produced raw materials (active ingredients and excipients). Although samples of finished products are tested periodically by the Drug Administration, there is no regular system of quality checking of raw materials, and WHO has unfortunately provided no help with this either.

To manufacture a medicine in its dosage form – such as a tablet, capsule, sachet, syrup, suspension, ointment or injection – one has to use a particular active ingredient which is also known as the 'bulk drug'. Bulk drug production is thus part of the chemical industry rather than the drug industry. Bulk drugs are known by their chemical or generic names and their producers do not enjoy the benefit of excessive profits through the symbiotic profit mechanism of brand names and patents. China, India, Brazil, Holland, and eastern and southern European countries are the main producers of bulk raw materials, and Bangladesh imports most of its raw materials from these countries.

Beximco and Sunipon Chemicals produce bulk paracetamol in Bangladesh. When paracetamol tablets produced by five large national and transnational companies from bulk paracetamol were analysed by independent researchers in May 1992, the products of both Beximco and Sunipon Chemicals had double the allowable quantity of the impurity P-aminophenol.

GPL was the first pharmaceutical company in Bangladesh to produce bulk ampicillin trihydrate. This was in 1989. It also produces bulk amoxycillin and cephalexin and will soon be marketing bulk diclofenac sodium. Analysis of bulk ampicillin manufactured by GPL (using spectrophotometric and gas chromatographic testing methods and high-pressure liquid chromatography) proved that it met British pharmacopoeia and US pharmacopoeia standards,[23] and the GPL products compare well with those of the bulk ampicillin trihydrate produced by Gist-Brocades of Holland and Antibioticos of Spain, both leading companies in this field.

To measure loss of potency, ascertain the duration of stability, and determine the expiry date of the products, the researchers performed accelerated heat-stability tests at 65° Centigrade for seven days. The duration of stability can safely be set at up to four years if the potency loss is within the 5 per cent limit. The results of the tests are given in Table 5.8.

Table 5.8:   Accelerated stability data of GPL's ampicillin trihydrate at 65° C

| Batch number | Initial results | | Results after 7 days | | Loss of potency |
	(assay)	(appearance)	(assay)	(appearance)	(percentage)
005/90	99.0	White	95.9	Unchanged	3.1
020 S 90	97.7	-	96.1	-	1.6
023 S 90	98.0	-	97.1	-	0.9
085/90	98.8	-	94.5	-	4.3
095/90	98.5	-	97.4	-	1.1
179/90	98.8	-	95.3	-	3.5

Source: Roy, J., et al, 'Pharmaceutical Analysis and Stability of Locally Manufactured Ampicillin Trihydrate'. *Indian Drugs*, Bombay, 1993.

Misleading drug promotion: a continuing problem

Leading companies also produce poor-quality medicine but to a lesser extent than smaller ones. However, their promotional materials frequently do not conform to WHO's *Ethical Criteria for Medicinal Drug Promotion*. In 1988, in their promotional materials for the Eskaycillin brand of ampicillin trihydrate (a package which included a free writing pad), SmithKline and French claimed a success rate of over 90 per cent for treatment of respiratory-tract infection, 100 per cent for cystitis, 95 per cent for gonorrhoea, 88 per cent for typhoid fever, 86 per cent for bacillary dysentery and 88.4 for bacterial enteritis. However, all the references that the company quoted were published in 1963 and 1964, when Beecham first marketed ampicillin under the brand name of Penbritin[24].

Ciprofloxin (brand name Neofloxin) is promoted by Beximco, a large national company, as 'highly effective in infectious diarrhoea like Traveller's Diarrhoea'.[25] There is no evidence that this claim is true.

The majority of misleading and fraudulent advertisements which appear in the daily newspapers and periodicals are placed by the manufacturers of homeopathic, Ayurvedic and Unani medicines. These advertisements claim 100 per cent success in curing sexual problems among young and newly-wed couples, obesity, asthma, eczema, psoriasis and other skin diseases, chronic dysentery, and so on. Advertisements also offer treatment for cancer, mental illnesses, heart diseases, diabetes, jaundice, tumours, sinusitis, leucorrhoea, leucoderma and baldness. Most of these problems do not have simple treatments, and in many cases allopathic cures do not exist. As the advertisements do not mention any names of drugs, the advertiser cannot be prosecuted under the Drug (Control) Ordinance 1982.[26] Because of loopholes in the law, only in seven out of 165 cases were advertisers found guilty of misrepresentation. As the penalty is nominal, offenders continue undeterred.[27] In 1993, there were 76 cases pending in the drug court against 17 traditional medicine manufacturers for illegal advertisements.[28]

Deceitful promotion by Ciba-Geigy

During 1988 and 1989, Ciba-Geigy encouraged consumers of the anti-tubercular drug rimactane (Rifampin) to 'buy three tablets, get one free'. They also distributed the drug widely to doctors through a campaign of special discount coupons.

Ciba-Geigy introduced the anti-depressants imipramine (brand name Tofranil) and amitriptyline into the USA in 1959 and 1961 respectively. Both drugs are also used for nocturnal enuresis in children, are well established and relatively safe and effective. In 1981, the company brought out another tetracyclic antidepressant, maprotiline (brand name Ludiomil), similar to amitriptyline but with a higher sedative effect and increased risk of convulsions. After five years of intense market promotion of Ludiomil, Ciba-Geigy had captured only 3 per cent of the US market for antidepressant drugs.[29] It then started exporting the drug to Third World countries, including Bangladesh.

When the company opened its factory in Bangladesh in the late 1980s, a marketing strategy for Ludiomil was planned at the firm's headquarters in Basel, Switzerland. The strategy was not just to promote Ludiomil, but to promote depression. Accordingly, on 19 May 1991, Ciba-Geigy (Bangladesh) held a large public health meeting at a five-star hotel, attended by senior doctors, influential members of society, and the press. Here the Bangladeshi marketing manager explained that such symptoms as insomnia and lack of energy and initiative were 'cardinal symptoms of depression'. The event was followed up with a campaign of advertising on peak-time television spots, on the radio and in the press, and by widespread distribution of a full-colour poster depicting a beautiful young girl with large sorrowful eyes, obviously in a depressed mood.[30] The television story began with the same girl sitting in her study, mindlessly turning the pages of a book and then moving on to a rocking chair. Finally an attractive voice announced, 'Depression is a disease'. Anyone suffering from depression was urged to seek advice from a doctor.

Doctors had already been briefed, and drug stores, seduced by the usual discount, had taken stocks of Ludiomil. Two months later, with the threat of legal action by the consumer organisation Health For All, the director of the Drug Administration stopped the 'public awareness campaign' in the broadcast and print media, by which time, according to Ciba-Geigy's own internal documentation, the company had nearly doubled its sales of Ludiomil.[31] The company continued to distribute a glossy brochure with the same picture as the one on the poster and a graph showing that 57 per cent of patients experienced a significant alleviation of depression after four days' treatment with Ludiomil, while only 15 per cent experienced an improvement with amitriptyline. An activity profile was also provided. This showed the relative performance of Ludiomil and amitriptyline as 'drive-enhancing', 'mood-brightening' and 'anxio-lytic' and depicted amitriptyline as inferior in every respect, particularly on its drive-enhancing record. Three references were mentioned: one from the *South African Medical Journal* of 1974 (Bangladesh did not recognise South Africa at the time), one from the German publication *Arztl Prax* of 1974 and another without a publisher's name. No medical institute in Bangladesh received these publications. In a country with a 26 per cent basic literacy rate in Bengali, how many people would be likely to read German? More-over, nowhere in the promotional materials or media advertisements did Ciba-Geigy mention that each 25 mg tablet of Ludiomil cost Taka 3 while a 25 mg tablet of amitriptyline cost only Taka 0.46: in other words, Ludiomil was six times more expensive.

Ciba-Geigy had clearly violated WHO's *Ethical Criteria* which state that 'promotional material should not be designed so as to disguise its real nature', and, furthermore, that 'psychotropic drugs should not be advertised to the general public'.[32]

Bangladesh is not the only country where TNCs are violating the WHO code. In a criminal investigation, the Grand Jury in New York subpoenaed Ciba-Geigy for misleading promotion of the pain-killer Volteran (diclofenac sodium) which used baseball celebrity Micky Mantle to endorse the product.[33]

Roche: champion bribe-giver

The Swiss TNC Roche has achieved an outstanding name for un-ethical promotion leading to irrational prescription. Among misused drugs, third-generation cephalosporin ceftriaxone, marketed by Roche under the brand name Rocephin, ranks very high.

Ceftriaxone is an antibiotic used for the treatment of serious bacterial infections (pneumococcus, group B-streptococci, gonocci and haemophilus influenzae) in babies, infants, older children and adults. Its significant characteristic is that it remains potent for (on average) 6.5 hours, which allows for less frequent dosing than other antimicrobial drugs.[34]

Research documented by Roche showed that for the treatment of meningitis, ceftriaxone achieved a similar outcome to conventional antimicrobial therapy using ampicillin alone or ampicillin plus chlor-amphenicol.[35] However, the per day treatment cost with ceftriaxone in Bangladesh is 20–30 times higher than the cost of conventional therapy, depending on the dose of Rocephin and the weight of the patient. Likewise, cure rates for treatment of gonorrhoea with single-dose ceftriaxone were similar to those achieved with penicillin-G-procaine.[36] But treatment with penicillin costs much less.

On the debit side, laboratory tests revealed haematologic abnormalities in 14.4 per cent of the volunteers tested.[37] One of these abnormalities, hypoprothrombinemic bleeding, calls for vitamin K to be administered (10 mg per week) to patients suffering from chronic hepatic disease or malnutrition when ceftriaxone therapy is initiated.[38] In Bangladesh, over 50 per cent of the population have less than a 2,000-calorie daily intake of food. Malnutrition and chronic hepatic disease are common. Abnormal liver chemistries were also observed.[39]

In short, ceftriaxone may be a useful medicine in the treatment of serious bacterial infections but it is very costly and is not recommended for prophylactic use in most cases because of the adverse reactions that may occur.

Ceftriaxone is not produced in Bangladesh but imported exclusively by a small office of Roche in Dhaka from the parent company in Switzerland. At the time of the drug's registration in 1989, the Roche representative assured the Drug Control Committee (upon whose recommendation the director of the Drug Administration registers a product) that the product would be promoted only to specialists and that utilisation data would be submitted to the Drug Administration. No utilisation data have so far been submitted. How did Roche, with only a small office in Dhaka, manage to turn Rocephin into a top seller among the most misused drugs within two years of its introduction into the market? Unethical promotion, coupled with bribery, were the tricks used.

Of all medical journals, the *British Medical Journal* (*BMJ*), is the best known among doctors in Commonwealth countries. Every doctor in Bangladesh has heard of the *BMJ*, but it would be reasonable to estimate that over 99 per cent of doctors never read the journal. The annual subscription for the *BMJ* is equivalent to one month's salary for a junior doctor. Senior doctors on high incomes who do not find the time to read medical journals consider it prestige-enhancing to have an occasional copy of the *BMJ* in the consulting room, and advertisements in the journal are always seen, though often erroneously, as scientific endorsement of the product advertised. Like other TNCs, Roche frequently presents selected copies of the *BMJ* and other journals to doctors as gifts. Companies promote their advertisements in these publications as if they were articles reporting on scientific research. Roche's advertisements for Rocephin are persuasive, claiming '24 hours bactericidal power –

Pathogens eliminated – No side effects – Well tolerated even in children'.[40] How wonderful!

Distinguished medical journals such as the *BMJ*, *The Lancet*, the *New England Journal of Medicine* and the *Journal of the American Medical Association* do not publish reports of industry-sponsored symposia but accept advertisements without critically evaluating them.[41] Pharmacologists have found that up to 25 per cent of advertisements in Australian publications contain unjustified claims.[42]

Roche introduced Rocephin to doctors in Bangladesh as a quick 'magic cure' for serious infections on the basis of a single daily injection, swiftly changing the promotion to 'twice a day works better and faster'. To facilitate promotion, Roche rented a beautiful house in a wealthy locality and converted it into a number of well-decorated chambers which were given free of charge to consultants, with the added benefit of easy access to a senior official in the health ministry.

Roche made an arrangement with a top Dhaka surgeon whereby he would write ten prescriptions for Rocephin daily in return for a cash payment of Taka 100,000 (US$2,500) at the end of the month. This is a very cost-effective way for Roche to achieve guaranteed sales and high profits.

Rocephin has claimed a place in every second prescription of many senior surgeons and paediatricians in Bangladesh. Some paediatricians prescribe it for every case of acute respiratory infection and many surgeons prescribe it as a prophylactic in all sorts of surgical cases, both major and minor. 'The promotional activities of the manufacturers have created a demand greater than actual needs', wrote the Expert Committee which prepared WHO's *The Selection of Essential Drugs* in 1977.[43] Roche's promotion of Rocephin is a classic example of this state of affairs.

Not only is Rocephin used for the wrong indications but it is not cost-effective either. The official price of a single dose in 1990 was just over US$16 but because of the Roche monopoly cartel the actual price is US$25, much more than the recommended maximum retail price. The cost of daily treatment with third-generation cephalosporin is almost 30 times that of first-generation oral cephalosporin and four times that of the second-generation cephalosporin injection. Authoritative pharmacologists confirm that the third-generation drug is often used for conditions in which less expensive antibiotics would provide adequate therapy.[44]

In March 1991, an article in *Time* magazine revealed that Roche paid doctors US$1,200 each to prescribe Rocephin to 20 hospital patients in exchange for minimal information on the result of the therapy.[45] Between 1986 and 1991, Roche paid between US$500 and US$2,500 as 'research grants' to each US physician willing to recommend Rocephin and other Roche products to other physicians who were in a position to include them in a hospital formulary. On investigation, the Office of the Inspector-General for Civil Fraud and Administrative Adjudication found that 'some doctors had not completed the research but had received the full payment and that in many cases the research had not been of any scientific value'.[46] Roche agreed to pay US$450,000 to the US Department of Health and Human Services as a penalty for improper inducements to physicians. However, a spokeswoman for Roche, Dane Donlon, said that the company's research grant for Rocephin was 'designed to educate doctors and pharmacists about the innovative use of the drug in severe infections', adding that the company '[did] not understand why the Office of the Inspector-General found the research findings of no value'.[47]

Dr Sidney Wolfe, director of the US Public Health Research Group who blew the whistle about Roche's actions referred to the so-called research inducements as 'a bribery campaign designed to induce prescribing'.[48] He had first been alerted to the situation when he received a telephone call on his 'bribery hot line' from a disease specialist in Florida who had been approached by Roche as a possible participant in December 1990.

How much Roche paid selected surgeons at the Institute of Cardiovascular Disease Research in Dhaka and the Bangladesh Institute of Research on Disorders of Endocrinology and Metabolism – besides presenting them with gold-cap Parker Pens with which to write their prescriptions for Rocephin – has not yet been made public, but it is known that payments were made. This kind of criminal behaviour is entirely consistent with the past record of Hoffman La Roche, which made its fortune during two world wars by selling heroin and morphine to the underworld.[49]

Other offenders

Organon promotes the oral capsule Tantum (50 mg of benzydamine hydrochloride) in Bangladesh as effective treatment for acute inflammation of the urogenital tracts in both sexes, as well as for inflammation of the respiratory tract, blood vessels and lymph vessels, oedematious conditions, post-traumatic and post-operative disorders, and dental problems.[50] In Europe, vaginal tablets rather than oral capsules of Tantum are recommended for vaginal conditions, and the list of indications for which the drug is applicable is much smaller.

Organon also promotes Anaroxyl (monosemicarbazone adrenochrome) tablets and injections for 'the prevention and treatment of surgical and non-surgical capillary bleeding and a dry field of operation'.[51] Furthermore, it claims that there are no known contraindications. Obviously, so long as the product remains within the Third World there will be no known contra-indications in the future either.

Anaroxyl was never registered for regular use in The Netherlands, Organon's home country, but in May 1986 it was registered 'for export only'. The product is not included in the 1989 *Directory of Registered Products* of The Netherlands, nor is there any mention of it in the 30th edition of *Martindale: The Extra Pharmacopoeia*.

National companies are also catching up with TNCs in their promotional activities, in some respects surpassing them. Beximco, the second-largest national company, gained approval for the recipe for omeprazole without clinical testing in Bangladesh. Furthermore, to beat its competitor, the company started marketing its own product Proceptin (omeprazole) without the product registration number.[52] With the introduction of vitamin B-complex syrup in large bottles, the same company told doctors, in its promotional literature, that many of their patients would enjoy taking Aristoplex syrup 'for its taste alone'.[53]

SmithKline and French was taken over by Transcom, the sole distributor of Nestlé products, in 1990, since when the pattern of fraudulent promotion has remained the same. The new management claims 100 per cent success in the treatment of tonsillitis and pneumonia with SK-MOX, their brand of amoxicillin trihydrate, and over 95 per cent success in cases of otitis media (inflammation of the middle ear), pharyngitis and bronchitis. Two references were given in the promotional material without the name of the articles and authors.[54]

The toll-free auto-dialer 'respiratory season hot line'[55] presented to doctors in the USA has not yet been introduced in Bangladesh, but gifts of pens, packets of coffee and sweets, calendars, pornographic videos and even refrigerators are not uncommon. All these help to build up the 'partnership' that companies claim will benefit both doctors and themselves. But most Bangladeshi doctors would be unwilling to accept the view of Professor Douglas Waud of the University of Massachusetts Medical School that such 'gifts' are in fact bribes. Dr Waud calculated that US drug companies are spending US$165 million a year on doctors 'gifts'.[56]

Improved prescribing patterns

In the context of the ever-increasing number of drugs on the world market and the unethical promotional practices of drug companies, the quality of a prescription depends in large measure on the continuing education of the doctor. This ought to include information on new diseases and changes in disease patterns, and on new drugs and the extent to which they differ from existing drugs in terms of safety, effectiveness, side-effects, adverse reactions and treatment cost. Yet this updating of doctors' knowledge, especially in the area of clinical pharmacology, is almost non-existent in most Third World countries, including Bangladesh. Most medical practitioners obtain their information on drugs from the drug companies themselves. Most medical journals in Bangladesh are published irregularly and are anyhow financed largely through drug companies' advertisements.

When reforms were introduced in Sri Lanka, the government failed to take immediate and appropriate measures to educate private and public sector doctors and medical students about the reforms, which was crucial for the survival and continuation of the policy. This mistake was repeated by the Bangladesh government in the 1980s.

However, even in the absence of continuing education on clinical pharmacology, and of an official national formulary, the number of drugs per prescription issued by doctors in general practice and specialist practice alike has decreased considerably. Between 1982 and 1990, there was a drop from five or six drugs per prescription to between two and four. The average number of medicines prescribed per patient in 1990 was 2.77 for general practitioners, 3.52 for paediatricians and 3.91 for other specialist consultants.[57] That this change occurred in Bangladesh was because of the non-availability of harmful or useless drugs since the introduction of the National Drug Policy and the replacement of most combination drugs by single-ingredient products.

In November 1992, the International Network for the Rational Use of Drugs in Bangladesh, in collaboration with the community medicine and pharmacology departments of four medical colleges, conducted a survey to assess drug-use patterns in the public sector for six common diseases: watery diarrhoea, dysentery with blood, helminthiasis (infestation with parasitic worms), pneumonia, acute respiratory infections and scabies. The survey was conducted at ten Thana Health Complexes (primary health care centres with an average of 31 hospital beds serving an average population of 250,000) and ten Union Subcentres (basic primary health care units serving an average population of 20,000). Thana Health Complexes are run by between nine and twelve doctors while Union Subcentres, which are essentially mother-and-child health care centres, are run by a medical assistant or a Lady Health Visitor.

The study[58] found that the average number of drugs per prescription was 1.4; 81 per cent of patients received drugs according to prescription and were given adequate information about the drugs dispensed to them; 85 per cent of the drugs were selected from the essential drugs list and 78 per cent were prescribed in generic names; 24.5 per cent of patients were treated with antibiotics (Table 5.9).

Doctors had given patients slightly more consultation time than medical assistants – on average, 60 seconds per patient, compared with 48 seconds. Only 36.5 per cent of patients had been given an adequate examination. Misuse of the anti-infective drug metronidazole was noted in 16.5 per cent of cases, since none of the patients for whom the drug was prescribed required it as part of their treatment. The prescribing habits of doctors and medical assistants were very similar.

Table 5.9: Drug use pattern for six common diseases and quality of care in rural out-patient departments in 1992

Indicators	Thana Health Complex	Union Sub-Centre
Average number of drugs prescribed per patient	1.44	1.48
Patients receiving antibiotics (percentage)	25	24
Patients prescribed metronidazole (percentage)	15	18
Drugs prescribed in generic name (percentage)	77	78
Drugs prescribed from essential drug list (percentage)	89	82
Patients treated according to defined standard (percentage)	43	39
Average consultation time per patient (seconds)	60	48
Patients receiving an adequate examination (percentage)	41	32
Drugs dispensed according to prescription (percentage)	80	82
Patients with adequate knowledge about their dispensed drugs (percentage)	80	82

Source: 'Results of drug use survey in Bangladesh', *Essential Drugs Monitor*, No. 16, World Health Organization, Geneva, 1993.

A comparison may be made with the situation in Pakistan. A survey conducted in 1994 among leading general practitioners in Karachi[59] showed that the average number of drugs prescribed per consultation was 4.86; 73.3 per cent of children were prescribed at least one antibiotic. Prescribing of harmful and inessential drugs was high among general practitioners: 40 per cent prescribed dipyrone (brand name Novalgin), 85 per cent of GPs had kaolin and pectin in syrup forms in their dispensaries, and 60 per cent frequently prescribed Lomotil (diphenoxylate hydrochloride) for diarrhoea. However, the average consultation time per patient, at just under three minutes, was considerably higher than in Bangladesh.

In Bangladesh, the NDP restricted non-life-saving drugs with a narrow safety margin to adult use only. Liquid forms of these drugs were deregistered to ensure that they were not given to children. In certain cases, syrups and suspensions in adult doses were not approved either, in order to reduce foreign-exchange wastage.

In one respect at least, children in Bangladesh are more fortunate than US children. Diphenoxylate hydrochloride (brand name Lomotil) and loperamide hydrochloride in syrup form (brand name Imodium) were banned in Bangladesh in 1982, whereas even in 1993 the US Public Citizen Committee had to continue to appeal to Dr David A. Kessler, Commissioner of the Federal Drugs Adminstration, to ban paediatric prescription and over-the-counter dosage forms of these drugs in the USA.[60] According to WHO, these drugs have no role in the treatment or management of diarrhoea in children, so there is no rationale for their production and sale in liquid and syrup forms for paediatric use.[61] Furthermore, diphenoxylate hydrochloride has potentially fatal side-effects on the central nervous system which may occur even at usual therapeutic dosages.[62]

The cost of medicines per illness in Bangladesh is on average Taka 122, and Taka 249.9 for terminal illness.[63] However, the average cost per prescription in Bangladesh is approximately half of the total costs incurred per sickness. The average cost of GPs' prescriptions is much less than that of specialists' prescriptions. In Pakistan the situation is similar: the mean cost per GP's prescription is Rupees 120, while for a paediatrician it is Rupees 160.

Specialists and inappropriate prescription

Prescription patterns reflect the frequency of medical representatives' visits, particularly high among medical teachers and busy consultants. Studies suggest that attendance at 'scientific' company-sponsored symposia and acceptance of pharmaceutical companies' publications 'alter physicians' prescribing practices and patient care', often resulting in their prescribing inappropriate and expensive drugs even for unapproved indications.[64] All doctors working for the Bangladesh government, including professors of medical institutes, are free to indulge in unlimited private practice. Doctors in a position of authority and influence are encouraged by drug companies to attend company-sponsored seminars in their own countries and abroad.

This practice is rife in industrialised countries. One survey in Canada revealed that 17 per cent of doctors had their travel expenses and conference fees paid by pharmaceutical companies and 3 per cent were presented with computer equipment.[65] Unfortunately, many symposium proceedings are later published in well-known journals with financing from the same sponsor; the *British Medical Journal*, *The Lancet*, the *New England Journal of Medicine* and the *Journal of the American Medical Association* are notable exceptions to the plethora of medical journals which publish drug companies' symposium proceedings (Table 5.10).

Table 5.10: Number of symposia proceedings published in selected journals.

Journals	Number of symposia proceedings published	
	1966–1979	1980–1989
American Journal of Cardiology	32	79
American Heart Journal	0	25
Hypertension	0	17
Circulation	3	11
American Journal of Medicine	18	67
American Journal of Obstetrics	0	10
British Journal of Anaesthesia	5	11
Cancer	6	13
Journal of Allergy Immunology (Clinical)	1	11
Kidney International	5	23
Transplantation Proceedings	6	56
British Medical Journal	0	0
New England Journal of Medicine	0	0
Lancet	0	0
Journal of the American Medical Association	0	0

Source: Bero, L. A. et al, 'The Publication of Sponsored Symposiums in Medical Journals', *New England Journal of Medicine*, 15 October, 1992.

These journals are then distributed free to other, less senior doctors to make sure that they too prescribe the new, often dubious products. Such publications also promote untested new technology. The prescriptions issued by senior physicians are immediately copied by juniors, and gradually by general practitioners and by unqualified doctors. This tendency is pronounced in Third World countries.

Drugs of doubtful value such as vinpocetine (brand name Cavinton, from Medimpex of Hungary), bencylane hydrogen fumerate (brand name Fludilat, from Organon) and oxpentifylline (brand name Trental, from Hoechst) appear remarkably frequently in the prescriptions written by senior teachers of neuromedicine. These drugs, at best of doubtful efficacy, at worst useless, remain in Bangladesh because of the persistent pressure by well-known senior professors for their retention.

Another concern is misprescription, such as the prescribing by gastroenterologists and other specialists of pancreatin enzyme (brand names Festal, from Hoechst, and Zymet, from Beximco) and oxiphenomonium bromide (brand name Antrenyl, from Ciba-Geigy) for indigestion. Some brands are more misused than others in the same category of drugs, obviously because of heavy promotion. Interestingly, drugs of doubtful efficacy are highly priced. A 250 mg tablet of ciprofloxacin, a useful drug but wrongly prescribed for ordinary fevers of two to three days' duration and for diarrhoea, cost Taka 12 in 1994, whereas cotrimaxazole cost just over Taka 1 per tablet. Similarly, a 300 mg ranitidine tablet was priced at Taka 4, while 20 mg of omeprazole cost Taka 14. Not only do bribes in the form of gifts, or travel and per diem expenses for attendance at seminars, increase the irrational prescription of drugs, they also add to the cost of these unnecessary drugs.

An extensive study of prescribing habits of GPs and paediatricians in Indonesia, undertaken in 1988 by the Indonesian Consumer Federation found that GPs wrote fewer drugs per prescription than paediatricians (Table 5.11).[66] Paediatricians also often wrote two or more antibiotics in the same prescription (in 21.1 per cent of cases, compared with 12.4 per cent for GPs). GPs prescribed two or more vitamins (15.8 per cent) and two or more antidiarrhoeal drugs (31.6 per cent) in the same prescription, a higher incidence than for paediatricians. But oral rehydration therapy (ORT), generally acknowledged to be the most important and effective form of treatment for diarrhoea, had been prescribed in only 16.03 per cent of all the cases.

Although the situation in Bangladesh is slightly better than that

Table 5.11: Number of drugs per prescription by general practitioners and paediatricians in Indonesia in 1988

Category of doctors	Number of doctors	1–2 drugs	3–4 drugs	5–6 drugs	7–9 drugs	10 + drugs	Total number of prescriptions	Average number of drugs per prescription
General Practitioners	650	411 (39.5%)	409 (39.4%)	150 (14.4%)	63 (6%)	6 (0.5%)	1039 (100%)	3.26
Paediatricians	300	263 (32.35%)	288 (35.4%)	187 (21.8%)	81 (10.0%)	3 (0.37%)	813 (100%)	3.69

Source: YLKI/ARDA, *Children's Drugs Prescribing Patterns: Case study of Indonesia,* 1988.

in Indonesia, inappropriate prescription of antibiotics for the treatment of diarrhoea in children persists. Most specialists and GPs in private practice, although aware of the advisability of using ORT, prescribe a wide range of broad-spectrum antibiotics such as nalidixic acid and furazolidone.[67]

Before the NDP, brands of clioquinol, such as Mexaform, Entero-vioform and Vioform, were so well known and widely available that doctors prescribed clioquinol as the first line of treatment for all types of diarrhoea, and self-prescription of the drug was also common. Since the banning of these products in 1982, nalidixic acid, a drug which pharmacology textbooks recommend mainly for the treatment of urinary-tract infections (commonly caused by Eschorichia coli, Proteus, Klebsiella and Pseudomonas Aeroginosa) has frequently been misprescribed by doctors for the treatment of diarrhoea.

However, in the outpatient departments of teaching hospitals, mostly managed by young doctors who are cautious about pre-scribing broad-spectrum antibiotics, 75 per cent of diarrhoea cases are treated with ORT.[68]

Inappropriate prescription of antibiotics – in respect of indications for disease or duration of application – is the most common symptom of bad prescribing habits. In 1986, an audit of a medical unit in a teaching hospital showed that 10 out of 13 antibiotic combinations used were ineffective or harmful.[69]

Professor Nurul Anwar of the Department of Pharmacology at Dhaka Medical College reported in 1992 that 79 per cent of prescriptions contained at least one error, resulting in overdose, undertreatment or adverse interaction.[70] He identifies aggressive promotion by drug companies as the main cause of bad prescription.

The extent of bad prescription is directly related to the health ministry's lack of concern for patients and its failure to make efforts on their behalf. A national formulary is one tool in the prevention of bad prescription and is a good aide in deciding the proper use of a particular drug. The NDP recommended that a national formulary should be published by 1983. It is yet to be published. The government made no attempt to communicate to consumers, through print or electronic media, the scientific and other reasons for the importance of a drug policy, the use of generic names, the control of treatment costs and, above all, non-drug therapy. The same attitude continues today.

Unfortunately, the problem of bad prescription is not even acknowledged by the president of the BMA, Dr M. A. Majed, a former ENT (ear, nose, throat) professor and principal of Dhaka Medical College, who received his postgraduate education in Britain. According to him, drug misuse is not caused by any deficiency in knowledge, and when a doctor appears to be prescribing irrationally, his intention is usually to cover all the possible diagnoses at the time and he is probably right to do so.[71]

Like doctors in industrialised countries, doctors in Bangladesh are keen to preserve their rights to clinical freedom and *laissez-faire* prescription but averse to a medical audit of their prescription habits. On 12 June 1990, the eighth anniversary of the NDP, the Bangladesh government introduced compulsory prescription for the four most frequently misused groups of drugs – antibiotics, narcotics, hormones (except contraceptives) and benzodiazepines – in the capital city, Dhaka, where there is no dearth of doctors.[72] Doctors were asked to collect prescription pads from the Drug Administration.[73]

Each prescription slip was in triplicate and bore the same serial number. The top sheet was for the patient, the second for the pharmacy, and the third for the doctor to retain. Spaces were given for various kinds of information to be recorded: the name of the doctor; the address and registration number of the practice: the name, age and address of the patient; major symptoms of the disease; drug specification and advice on diet and lifestyle. The health ministry intended to extend the system to cover the whole of Bangladesh in phases, after evaluation of the experiment in Dhaka.

The BMA refused to endorse the system. Slogans calling for clinical freedom and drugs to be available on prescription only are one thing, but a medical audit is another matter. Who wants accountability?

The most misused drug in Bangladesh is undoubtedly diclofenac sodium, for which Ciba-Geigy's brand name is Volteran. Diclofenac is produced by many large and small national companies beside Ciba-Geigy. Unchecked promotion has meant that it has come to be used as an ordinary pain-relieving drug in both urban and rural areas, rather than for post-operative or serious arthritic pain. In the last half of 1992, at Gonoshasthaya Kendra, six male patients had to have operations for perforations after taking diclofenac tablets. None of them had a previous history of suffering from ulcers. In 1993, a large number of perforations of the alimentary systems, following ingestion of these drugs, made newspaper headlines.[74]

It is not that doctors are unaware of the dangers. When prescribing diclofenac, they also frequently prescribe ranitidine or cimetidine (a smaller number prescribe simple antacid), a practice which must be prompted by medical representatives in an attempt to prevent ulceration and/or perforation. Besides promotion, another reason for the fast-expanding use of diclofenac is its low price, which is of course due to the drug-pricing policy. In terms of price, a 25 mg diclofenac tablet is cheaper than 500 mg of paracetamol, but it may cost one's life.

When a new drug is registered in Third World countries its potential risks are rarely known. Quality testing is always difficult as local laboratories may be unfamiliar with the testing procedures required for the drug and with new chemical entities if these are not included in the regular pharmacopoeia or *Martindale: The Extra Pharmacopoeia*. Furthermore, the concept of surveillance and evaluation of new drugs after they come on to the market is unknown in Third World countries. WHO should take responsibility either for preventing the export of unapproved and dubious drugs to Third World countries or for ensuring that drug-testing laboratories in the countries are equipped with the necessary technology for quality testing and that their technicians are given full instructions about testing and evaluation procedures.

Notes

1. Chetley, A., 'Essentials for Health: Ensuring Equitable Access to Drugs, Media Briefing No. 11, Panos, London 1994.

2. *Bangladesh Financial Survey 1990/1991*, Ministry of Finance, Government of Bangladesh, Dhaka, 1991.

3. Brigadier Mukhlesur Rahman Khan, Director, Drug Administration, Dhaka, personal communication with author on 4 April 1993.

4. Khan, Naheed, 'Drug Prices', *The Dawn*, Karachi, 7 February 1993.

5. Kintanar, Q. L., Marketing Policy: Focus on The Philippines', in *Prescription for Change*, Philippine Center for Investigative Journalism/Dag Hammarskjöld Foundation, Sweden, 1992.

6. Ibid.

7. 'Philippine Generics Act – little impact?', *Scrip*, London, 29 November 1991.

8. Roy, J., 'The Menace of Substandard Drugs', *World Health Forum*, Vol. 15, No. 4, 1994.

9. Roy, J., Saha, P., Rahman, A. and Zakaria, M., 'Quality of Marketed Paracetamol Tablets in Bangladesh – An Analytical Overview', Department of Pharmacy, Jahangirnagar University/Institute of Public Health, Dhaka, 1992, (mimeo).

10. Roy, J., 'Current Status of the Quality of Marketed Drugs', Department of Pharmacy, Jahangirnagar University, Dhaka, 1992, (mimeo).

11. Safiullah, S. and Roy, J., 'Quality of Drugs in Bangladesh', *Weekly Bichitra*, Dhaka, 24 October 1986.

12. Roy, J., 'Current Status of the Quality of Marketed Drugs', op. cit.

13. The Drugs (Control) Ordinance, Government of People's Republic of Bangladesh, Dhaka, 1982.

14. Gilman, A. G., et al. (eds), *Goodman and Gilman's 'The Pharmacological Basis of Therapeutics'*, 8th edition, Pergamon Press, 1990.

15. Roy, J., Saha, P., Rahman, A. and Zakaria, M., op. cit.

16. Gilman, A. G., et al., op. cit.

17. Patel, Tara, 'Real juice, pure fraud', *New Scientist*, London, 21 May 1994.

18. Lentin, B., 'Report of the Commission of Inquiry: Deaths of Patients in JJ Hospital at Bombay in January-February, 1986 due to alleged reaction of drugs', Government of India, 1988.

19. Silverman, M., Lydecker, M. and Lee, P. R., *Bad Medicine: The Prescription Drug Industry in the Third World*, Stanford University Press, California, Berkeley, 1992.

20. Pfizer withdrawal notice advertisement, 'Diamine Penicillin 12 Lac Unit', in *Daily Ittefaq, Dainik Bangla* and *Bangladesh Observer*, 22 and 23 March 1989.

21. For example, 'Spurious drugs worth Tk 2cr. (20 million) seized', *Bangladesh Observer*, Dhaka, 27 September 1993; 'Search in wholesale drugs market of Mitford: Counterfeit drugs worth Taka 20 million found', *Dainik Bangla*, Dhaka, 27 September 1993; 'Spurious tonic seized in city', *Daily Star*, Dhaka, 28 September 1993.

22. 'Business of spurious life saving drugs', *Ittefaq*, Dhaka, 9 July 1993.

23. Roy, J., Mohammad, G. and Banu, A., 'Pharmaceutical Analysis and Stability of Locally Manufactured Ampicillin Trihydrate', *Indian Drugs*, Bombay, May 1993.

24. 'Eskaycillin (Ampicillin Trihydrate BP): a first move to combat infection', SmithKline & French, Dhaka ESK-Rx-A/86, 1988.

25. 'Treatment of G.I. infection sometimes considered to be difficult', show-card for Neofloxin (Ciprofloxacin USP), Beximco Pharmaceuticals, Dhaka, 1992.

26. The Drugs (Control) Ordinance 1982, op. cit.

27. 'New law required to stop vulgar promotion of traditional systems of medicine', *Daily Janakantha*, Dhaka, 19 July 1993.

28. 'No quality control measures for Unani, Ayurvedic and Homeopathic Medicines', *Ittefaq*, Dhaka, 2 October 1993.

29. '1986 anti-depressant use in US', *Scrip*, London, 24 February 1988.

30. Roy, J., Rahman, M. and Rafiquzzanan, M., 'Promotion of Medicines in Bangladesh: Unethical case studies and their impact on the society', Department of Pharmacy, Jahangirnagar University, Dhaka, 1992, (mimeo).

31. Ibid.

32. WHO, *Ethical Criteria for Medicinal Drug Promotion*, Geneva, 1988.

33. 'Crackdown on Ciba-Geigy's US Promotion', *Scrip*, London, 25 September 1991.

34. Beam, T. R., 'Ceftriaxone: a beta lactamase stable, broad-spectrum cephalosporin with an extended half-life', Hoffmann La Roche, Basle, 1987.

35. Ibid.

36. Ibid.

37. Ibid.

38. Ibid.

39. A significant portion of Ceftriaxone is excreted through the hepatobiliary tract. The observed abnormal liver chemistries were alkaline phosphatase, SGOT and SGPT. An even higher rate of SGOT was observed in 7.2 per cent of the paediatric patients.

40. Advertisement by F. Hoffman-La-Roche Ltd., Basle, Switzerland, *British Medical Journal*, 22 September 1990.

41. Bero, L. A., Galbraith, A. and Rennie, D., 'The Publications of Sponsored Symposiums in Medical Journals', *The New England Journal of Medicine*, 15 October 1992.

42. 'MaLAM Australia targets Syntex and Janssen?', *Scrip*, London, 27 August, 1993.

43. WHO, *The Selection of Essential Drugs*, Technical Report Series 615, World Health Organization, Geneva, 1977.

44. Mandell, G. L. and Sandle, M. A., 'Antimicrobial Agents', in Gilman et al. (eds), *Goodman and Gilman's The Pharmacological Basis of Therapeutics*, 8th edition, Pergamon Press, 1990.

45. Purvis, Andrew, 'Cheaper can be better', *Time*, 16 March 1991.

46. Charatan, Fred B., 'Drug company settles over antibiotic claim', *British Medical Journal*, 17 September 1994.

47. Ibid.

48. 'Roche pays to settle OIG fraud claim', Sc*rip*, London, 16 September 1994.

49. Braithwaite, John, *Corporate Crime in the Pharmaceutical Industry*, Routledge and Kegan Paul, 1983.

50. 'Tantum: Swelling and Pain', promotional stationery, Organon (Bangladesh), Dhaka, 1993.

51. 'Anaroxyl – 5 good reasons why they choose Anaroxyl', Organon (Bangladesh) Ltd, Dhaka, 1990.

52. 'For extra profit – once again unnecessary drugs are being manufactured and marketed', *Ajker Kagoj* (Bengali daily newspaper), Dhaka, 14 June 1993.

53. Muktadir, A., 'Dear Doctor', Beximco Pharmaceuticals, Dhaka, 20 March 1993.

54. 'Clinical response of an antibiotic depends on the availability of the drug at the site action', promotional showcard , SmithKline & French (Bangladesh), 1993.

55. Klien, M., 'Novel gifts from pharmacetical companies', *New England Journal of Medicine*, 13 May 1993.

56. Waud, D. R., 'Pharmaceuticals promotion – a free lunch', *New England Journal of Medicines*, 30 July 1992.

57. UBINIG, 'Use and Abuse of Children's Medicine', Dhaka, 1990, (mimeo).

58. 'Results of drug use survey in Bangladesh', *Essential Drugs Monitor*, No. 10, World Health Organization, Geneva, 1993.

59. Ahmed, S. T., 'An inquiry into prescribing patterns of family physicians in Karachi', Baqai Institute of Health Sciences, Karachi, 1994 (MPH thesis).

60. Ahmad, S. R., Wolfe, S. M. and Lurie, P., 'Citizen's petition for a ban and/or relabelling of antidiarrhoeal drugs to David A. Kessler, Commissioner, Food and Drug Administration', *Public Citizen*, Washington DC, 7 January 1993.

61. WHO, 'The Rational Use of Drugs in the management of acute diarrhoea in children', World Health Organization, Geneva, 1990.

62. Ibid.

63. Khan, M. R., 'Health Care Financing in Bangladesh', in *Bangladesh Faces the Future*, Koht Norbye, Ole David (ed), University Press Ltd, Dhaka, 1990.

64. Bero, L. A., Galbraith, A. and Rennie, D., 'The Publications of Sponsored Symposiums in Medical Journals', *New England Journal of Medicine*, op. cit.

65. Lexchin, Joel, 'Percentage of Ontario physicians accepting benefits from pharmaceutical companies', Pharmaceutical Inquiry of Ontario, 1990.

66. YLKI/ARDA, 'Children's Drugs Prescribing Patterns: Case Study of Indonesia, Final Report, 1988–89', (mimeo).

67. UBINIG, op. cit.

68. Ibid.

69. Rashid, H., Chowdhury, S. A. R. and Islam, N., 'Pattern of Antibiotic Use in Two Teaching Hospitals', *Tropical Doctor*, London, October 1986.

70. Anwar, A. K. M. N., 'Towards Rational Drug Precribing' (mimeo), presented in the seminar 'Role of Mass Media in Rational Prescription of Drugs' held in Dhaka, 2–3 November 1992.

71. Chetley, A., 'From Policy to Practice', IOCU, Penang, 1992.

72. 'Prescription of 4 types of drugs effective in city', *Bangladesh Times*, Dhaka, 13 June 1990.

73. 'Special Notification to prevent misuse of drugs', Drug Adminstration, Government of the People's Republic of Bangladesh, Dhaka, 18 July 1990. Advertisements were published in *Bangladesh Observer* of 23 July 1990, and many other newspapers.

74. 'Incidence of perforations are throughout the country: 59 died in six districts', *Daily Sangbad*, Dhaka, 22 July 1993.

6

WHO's role: ambiguity and contradictions

In supporting efforts to develop national drug policies based on the sensible and safe use of a restricted number of drugs, and in facing up to the might of the pharmaceutical industry, WHO clearly has a crucial leadership role to play. In some respects its leadership has been strong, but this has not been consistent.

It has not given unambiguous support to national initiatives. In the case of Bangladesh, the WHO representative in Dhaka, Dr Z. Sestak, neither congratulated the Bangladesh government on enacting the NDP nor offered any services to make the policy effective. When asked about his silence, he said that comment could only be made by the regional office in Delhi and the head office in Geneva. It was also most astonishing that Dr Halfdan Mahler, WHO's Director-General, did not send a letter of congratulations or support for the successful implementation of the policy. It had, after all, been Dr Mahler who had declared at the 28th World Health Assembly in April 1975 that it was important to assist countries in formulating and implementing national drug policies.

It was fortunate for Bangladesh that the drug industry appeared not to notice WHO's silence. It would otherwise have been very difficult to defend the policy as people thought of the NDP as the mirror image of WHO's policy on drugs.

Dr Mahler came to Bangladesh to attend the 35th session of WHO's South-East Asian regional meeting on 14 September 1982. In the course of inaugurating the session, the health minister, Shamsul Huq, reiterated Bangladesh's commitment to reaching all citizens with health care as early as possible to reflect WHO's goal of Health for All by the year 2000. He also informed the audience of Bangladesh's new drug policy.

In his speech, Dr Mahler praised the Bangladesh government for its commitment to Health for All and for being the first country in the region to have a health charter, but he did not comment on the drug policy. Asked about this by a journalist, he said: 'Your government is to make the policy and WHO's main concern is that the people get the medicine.'[1] Pressed by another journalist on the same subject, Dr Mahler once again avoided a direct reply, saying only that it was for the government to decide policies for the people.[2] The industry-sponsored weekly *The Pulse* published an article entitled 'The sermon on the mount' about Dr Mahler's speech, in which it pointed out his absence of comment on the drug policy.[3] However, in a closed session after the media had left, Dr Mahler congratulated the minister for his courage in starting to put the country's drug house in order.

WHO's actions in other respects also raise questions as to its real intentions and motives.

Dr Zafrullah Chowdhury wrote to Dr Sestak on 5 September 1980, asking for his permission to translate and print *The Selection of Essential Drugs* into Bengali. After receiving several reminders, Dr Sestak replied on 23 April 1981, asking Dr Chowdhury not to take any action to translate and publish the document as he had not yet heard from WHO's head office.[4] Then, on 9 June 1981, he again wrote to Dr Chowdhury, informing him that the WHO regional office in Delhi (not the head office) regretted its inability to consider the request as Gonoshasthaya Kendra was a non-governmental organisation.[5]

In March 1994, WHO published a booklet entitled *Selected References on Essential Drugs*.[6] This listed documents on national drug policies in, among other places, the Andean countries of South America, Myanmar, the Philippines and Papua New Guinea, but not a single document on the Bangladesh policy was referred to in the booklet.

Slow progress with international drug marketing code

Dr Mahler was always very vocal about the drug industry's excessive promotional practices and the 'double standards' it employed in marketing drugs.[7] WHO was mandated to formulate an International Drug Marketing Code in May 1978.[8]

The USA withdrew from the International Labour Organization (ILO) in 1978 on the grounds that it was becoming 'highly politicised' (a justification which, in 1987, the USA also gave for its withdrawal from the United Nations Educational, Scientific and

Cultural Organization, UNESCO). This action made WHO take fright. By this time, Dr Mahler had become a shrewd politician and decided to slow down the pace of reform. WHO had a meeting on infant feeding in 1979 but it was not until 1981 that the World Health Assembly adopted an International Code of Marketing of Breast Milk Substitutes, in the face of US opposition. The International Baby Food Action Network (IBFAN), a loose coalition of NGOs formed in 1979, played a crucial role in pressing for the adoption of the code.

Spurred by this success, 50 participants from 27 countries formed Health Action International (HAI), a coalition modelled on IBFAN, at the end of May 1981. HAI's objectives include bringing an end to the 'commercial anarchy of prescription drug competition' and 'patent protection of most essential drugs', progressive replacement of proprietary brands with generic drugs, and the development of regional or national production and bulk-buying arrangements.[9]

The International Federation of Pharmaceutical Manufacturers Associations (IFPMA), having learnt its lesson from the campaign against breast milk substitutes, was worried that it could be similarly outmanoeuvred over drug marketing. It therefore took the decision to pre-empt a WHO code and in March 1981 announced its own Code of Pharmaceutical Marketing Practices. Subsequently, WHO chose to recommend endorsement of the IFPMA's code, disregarding its constitutional mandate to decide its own regulations on pharmaceutical marketing. Its Executive Board approved this line of action, stating that 'moral force' might be more effective than 'legal pressure'.[10]

At the 35th World Health Assembly in May 1982, a large number of Third World countries called for formal adoption of the WHO code. The Dutch representative, moreover, urged that this was necessary 'to prevent serious problems in which the good name of our organisation might be at stake'.[11] Despite these appeals, Dr Mahler made no attempt to carry the WHO-sponsored code through successive World Health Assemblies. However, in November 1985, WHO organised a special five-day conference of experts from the drug industry, consumer groups and government agencies in Nairobi. The conference inspired a determination to solve the world's drug problems through a new spirit of collaboration.

The dialogue ended with a declaration which Dr Mahler said embodied 'the spirit of Nairobi', and the conference was given an assurance that the subject would be decided upon at the next World Health Assembly in May 1986.[12] However, on this occasion nothing of significance took place. According to a British commentator: 'The mountain had laboured and brought forth a mouse. A very small mouse.'[13]

On 13 May 1988, the 41st World Health Assembly finally adopted the *Ethical Criteria for Medicinal Drug Promotion* as a formal resolution. It urged member states to take appropriate measures but at the same time made it clear that 'the criteria do not constitute legal obligations'.[14]

In addition to the *Ethical Criteria*, WHO also published *Guidelines for Developing National Drug Policies* in 1988.[15] However, very little effort was made to distribute these publications among medical practitioners and medical institutions in Third World countries. As Health Action International pointed out in 1992, it is therefore not surprising that the *Ethical Criteria* had had 'minimal impact on the standard of promotional practice worldwide'.[16]

In 1993, Unicef in Bangladesh took the initiative to translate the *Ethical Criteria* into Bengali and distribute copies among doctors and consumer groups.[17]

Clearly, WHO local offices are not very active in distributing their own publications: quite the reverse. The resident WHO representative in Bangladesh went so far as to state in 1992 that a national drug policy encouraged the smuggling of drugs.[18] (It is common knowledge that spices and saris are smuggled into Bangladesh from India, but this is not reported in the newspapers as frequently as the seizure and destruction of banned medicines such as Phensedyl – a combination cough mixture of codeine phosphate, ephedrine and promethazine hydrochloride – which is frequently smuggled into the country from India.)[19]

Such utterances have strengthened the anti-NDP lobby, which, with the change of government in 1991, has become very active again and has succeeded in changing some of the NDP's provisions (see Chapter 7).

Failure to speak out

Why is WHO not more consistently open in its support of the selection of essential drugs, the international drug marketing code and national drug policies?

The USA has consistently opposed WHO's policies on drugs in the interests of its own TNCs. Recently it changed its position on the development of national drug policies in relation to Third World countries only. During the 45th World Health Assembly in Geneva in 1992, the US delegation opposed an amendment to a policy statement on essential drugs, which proposed that all member states should take steps to implement the concept of essential drugs in their national policies in order to expand access and affordability. The US delegation forced the house to add the words 'where appropriate' to the amendment, to make sure that such resolutions have selective application only.[20]

What prevents WHO from speaking its mind openly? Is it because of the USA's reluctance to endorse its policies? Is it that the withdrawal of the USA from UNESCO arouses fear that it will likewise withdraw from WHO if the organisation takes definitive action on drugs without its concurrence? This would be a major financial blow as the USA contributes almost 25 per cent of the total WHO budget (another 20 per cent being contributed by Germany and Japan together).[21]

There are other possible explanations. WHO's staff consists primarily of doctors, from both Third World and industrialised countries, who are skilled in the scientific diagnosis and treatment of diseases but rarely show concern for social and environmental factors. Most of them fail to appreciate that a disease such as tuberculosis is an indicator of social inequality or that malnutrition and insanitary conditions contribute significantly to the incidence of the most common diseases of the Third World. They are unwilling to analyse these problems from a political or economic point of view.

WHO always takes an apolitical, neutral stand and, in adherence to its principle of non-interference, refrains from mentioning colonialism, neo-colonialism and imperialism, all of which have played a significant role in the causation and spread of diseases among the exploited and oppressed people of the world.[22] As the *British Medical Journal* has pointed out, 'WHO should be doing more to tackle the root cause of most diseases – poverty – and doing more to improve infrastructure of health care in the developing world.'[23]

Such action as WHO has taken on drugs is typical of the technological approach to health problems with which medical officers working for WHO feel familiar and comfortable. Doctors understand drugs in so far as they know about prescription and usage, efficacy and quality, but they do not apply their minds to the problems of how drugs reach the people who need them most. They do not realise that the class character and political will of the government determine the affordability and provision of essential drugs.

Nowhere in its documents does WHO clearly state that its essential drugs list is for both the private and the public sector. Moreover, WHO has not even highlighted the views of its own experts on this subject and allowed these to gain public attention. By the end of the 1980s the drug industry had come to accept, albeit reluctantly, the essential drugs strategy for the public or welfare sector but insisted that the private sector should be left to market forces and to the clinical wisdom of doctors. This provoked a sharp response from Professor Olikoye Ransome-Kuti, former health minister of Nigeria: 'Drugs are meant for diseases not sectors. If you can demonstrate to me that the diseases affecting people in the private sector are different to those affecting people in the public sector we shall adjust the list accordingly.'[24]

Although Professor Ransome Kuti was the president of WHO's Executive Board for many years, he did not succeed in incorporating his arguments into WHO's essential drugs policy statements. Dr Mahler and his successor, Dr Hiroshi Nakajima, made the rules. Whether this was done in ignorance or in collusion with the industry needs to be investigated before essential drugs policies can be fully implemented in Third World countries. In the absence of a clear declaration by WHO, plenty of room exists for easy penetration of ineffective and harmful drugs, first into the private sector and then into the public hospitals and the primary health care (PHC) sector. In reality, inessential drugs eat up a large proportion of the PHC sector drug budget.

WHO is known for its 'fixation on medical technology – vaccines, drugs and doctors – [and] its unwillingness to grapple with the practicalities of delivering health care'.[25] It does not state clearly that disease is not merely the consequence of poor health services and that the provision of primary health care alone does not bring better health. To break the chain responsible for diseases among the poor requires a political decision to act. To publish materials and then not to distribute them widely; to produce documents on drug policy but not to defend them actively, as in the case of Bangladesh's National Drug Policy: these contradictions reflect a political decision *not* to act. They are also examples of WHO's double standards and its dubious role. Moreover, the organisation 'escapes the moderating influence of public accountability and scrutiny from the international press'.[26]

WHO's concern for quality control of drugs, irrespective of whether they are produced by local or transnational manufacturers, is well known. The organisation does in fact occasionally provide consultants on quality control to Third World countries. WHO's first Certification Scheme on Good Practices in the Manufacture and Quality Control of Drugs was adopted in 1969, and in 1988 it introduced a Certification Scheme on the Quality of Pharmaceutical Products moving in International Commerce'.[27]

The scheme is only for finished products, not for raw materials, and certificates are issued in the required WHO format by the drug controller in the particular exporting country. It is worth noting that many drug controllers in Third World countries, including India, are not technically qualified.

Furthermore, WHO does not have its own testing facilities anywhere in the region; nor is it linked with any independent laboratory. It has no means of collecting drug samples regularly. The certificate does not provide any information on the academic qualifications and experience of personnel engaged in regular testing of manufactured products according to European or North American pharmacopoeial standards. Nor does it give any information on the amount of fully functioning equipment in the quality assurance department of the producer, the date of the last inspection of the factory by qualified technical personnel from the drug administration, or whether the company has been reprimanded or penalised for production of substandard drugs or unethical promotional activities during the previous five years.

No matter how grand or authentic it sounds, WHO's certification scheme is nothing more than a free sales certificate in WHO format. Free sales certificates were introduced as a means of serving the vested interests of transnational drug companies. The system is approved by WHO and provides a camouflage for manufacturers and suppliers which expedites registration of drugs in Third World countries. This is definitely not in the interests of Third World countries or individual consumers. But the scheme fits well with WHO's 'apolitical' and 'neutral' stand and its principle of 'non-interference'.[28]

Infiltration of WHO by TNCs

Transnational companies have cultivated friendly relationships with UN agencies since the 1960s. They have enjoyed a special status in their relationship with the Food and Agricultural Organization (FAO) through FAO's Industry Co-operative Programme (ICP) since 1967. Through this programme, they have had a strong influence on FAO policy, even to the extent of intervening in the choice of articles in the FAO publication *Ideas and Action*. Professor Eric Jacoby, who worked for FAO for many years, wrote in 1977: 'Through their representatives on the Central Committee of the FAO/ICP ... [they have gained] valuable information on forthcoming investment opportunities. Ever since ICP has become an integral part of the UN System, FAO actually functions as an agent for the transnational corporations in the underdeveloped world.'[29]

The first WHO Expert Committee on Essential Drugs did not include any representatives from the drug industry. Dr Hiroshi Nakajima, then Head of the Drug Policies and Management Division of WHO, who acted as the secretary of the committee, had previously worked for Hoffman La Roche. Although a very capable person, he could not prevent the Expert Committee from producing a document that was highly detrimental to the interests of TNCs. After this, to ensure better support for the industry, the Expert Committee started to include representatives from the IFPMA, the World Federation of Proprietary Medicine Manufacturers, the Commonwealth Pharmaceutical Association and the International Pharmaceutical Federation. The title of WHO's publication also changed quietly from *The Selection of Essential Drugs* to *The Use of Essential Drugs*, and the content of the document became less controversial and more apolitical.[30] While representatives from the pharmaceutical industry became members of the various expert committees, representatives from Health Action International, the International Organisation of Consumers' Unions and the Public Citizen Health Research Group have always been excluded from such committees. Paid employees of drug companies are recruited as advisors and consultants even when WHO is collaborating with the Council for International Organisations of Medical Sciences.[31]

IFPMA was given NGO status within WHO in 1971, overruling the recommendations of the commission responsible for advising on this matter.[32] This status makes it easy for IFPMA to have access to various WHO expert committees and consultative meetings, to make the acquaintance of representatives from member states, and to acquire detailed information about the background of those attending and insight into their thinking. By contrast, Third World governments do not usually send national experts to such consultations, mainly due to financial constraints, and have to rely instead on their embassies to represent them. (Even at WHO's annual meetings, Third World countries are represented by, at the most, two or three members, including the health minister as the team leader.) Embassies have a skeleton staff who are not usually technically qualified and are not in a position to attend all such meetings. Consequently, Third World countries are deprived of contacts, information and gossip, while TNCs acquire information which provides a crucial advantage in formulating strategies.

TNCs with participatory or observer status are able to acquire advance copies, not only of agendas, but also of the speeches of some Third World delegates. If the industry finds a speech is helpful to its cause directly or indirectly, or at least would create a counter current leading to confusion during the discussion of an agenda item against their interests, it arranges for the speech to be published in friendly newspapers. Thus prominence is given to a delegate who is unknowingly harming Third World interests.

Furthermore, WHO occasionally recruits personnel who have strong links with the industry and promote its interests rather than the ideals of WHO. Dr D. C. Jayasuriya, a Sri Lankan lawyer, was hired jointly by the IFPMA and the US Pharmaceutical Manufacturers Association (PMA) from May 1984 to January 1985 to write a book discrediting Bangladesh's National Drug Policy. 'I have written this monograph with a sense of disillusionment', he wrote. 'Bangladesh, I feel, is a country of lost opportunity.'[33] Dr Jayasuriya was also commissioned by WHO as a consultant on a number of occasions, notably during the Nairobi conference of experts in 1985. The IFPMA and PMA distributed copies of his book widely, promoting it as a publication by a Third World author who understood Bangladesh. At this time Dr Jayasuriya was a member of WHO's panel of temporary advisors.

Another example is Gerald D. Moore, a US citizen who has worked for WHO since the late 1980s and whose integrity has repeatedly been questioned. He was alleged to have made personal profits from supplying drug kits to Africa and to have enjoyed substantial 'kickbacks' from the drug industry.[34] In early 1990, Moore proposed the abolition of the drug registration system in Kenya, and he also cleverly misrepresented WHO in Zimbabwe. He was suspended on a number of occasions but always reinstated. Dr John Dunne, Director of the Drug Management and Policies (DMP) division, asked in 1994 whether Moore's behaviour 'could ... be regarded in any circumstance as admissible and worthy of WHO'[35]

It may justifiably be asked whose interests WHO is serving.

Notes

1. 'WHO Regional Meet to Strengthen Cooperation & Medicare to all as early as possible', *Bangladesh Times*, 15 September 1982.

2. 'Mahler lauds drug policy', *Bangladesh Observer*, Dhaka, 15 September 1982.

3. 'The sermon on the mount: Dr Mahler hails Health Policy, avoids comments on Drug Policy', *The Pulse*, 20 September 1982

4. Correspondence between Dr Z. Sestak, WHO Representative in Bangladesh, and Dr Zafrullah Chowdhury between 5 September 1980 and 15 May 1982.

5. Ibid.

6. Documentation Centre, APED, 'Selected references on essential drugs', WHO/DAP.94, World Health Organization, Geneva, March 1994.

7. *Multinational Monitor*, August 1982, op. cit.

8. Quoted in Melrose D., *Bitter Pills: Medicines and the Third World Poor*, Oxfam, Oxford, 1982.

9. HAI Press Release, 29 May 1981, quoted in Chetley, A., A *Healthy Business – World Health and the Pharmaceutical Industry*, Zed Books, 1990.

10. Hardon, A., 'Consumers versus Producers: Power Play Behind the Scenes', in *Drugs Policy in Developing Countries*, Zed Books, 1992.

11. Dr Sikket's intervention recorded in WHO/A35/A/SR/5, quoted in Melrose, D., *Bitter Pills: Medicines and the Third World Poor*, Oxfam, Oxford, 1982.

12. 'Rational Use of Drugs: Cooperation Prevails at WHO Conference in "Spirit of Nairobi" ', WHO Press Release, Geneva, 3 December 1985.

13. Milton Silverman in Silverman, M., Lydecker, M. and Lee, P. R., *Bad Medicine: The Prescription Drug Industry in the Third World*, Stanford University Press, California, 1992.

14. *Ethical Criteria for Medicinal Drug Promotion*, WHO, Geneva, 1988.

15. *Guidelines for Developing National Drug Policies*, WHO, Geneva, 1988.

16. 'HAI International Meeting on Impact of WHO Ethical Criteria for Medicinal Drug Promotion', Geneva, 27–29 April 1992.

17. Dr Agnes Guyon, UNICEF, Bangladesh, personal communication, 3 February 1993.

18. 'Drug policy encourages smuggling of drugs: WHO RR', *The Pulse*, Dhaka, 27–29 June 1992.

19. 'Phensedyl Syrup seized, one held', *Bangladesh Observer*, Dhaka, 18 April 1993, and 'Three arrested with Phensedyl', *Banglabazaar Patrika*, Dhaka, 22 May 1993, are but two examples of frequent news items in various dailies and weeklies.

20. 'Word games at World Health Assembly', *The Drug Monitor*, Quezon City, July/August 1992.

21. Silverman, M., Lydecker, M. and Lee, P. R., *Bad Medicine: The Prescription Drug Industry in the Third World*, Stanford University Press, California, Berkeley, 1992.

22. Turshen, M. and Thébaud, A., 'International Medical Aid', in *Monthly Review*, New York, December 1981.

23. Godlee, Fiona, 'WHO at the crossroads', *British Medical Journal*, 1 May 1993.

24. WHO, 'An Interview with Nigeria's Minister of Health', *Essential Drugs Monitor*, No. 12, Geneva, 1991.

25. Godlee, Fiona, op. cit.

26. Ibid.

27. *Guidelines for Developing National Drug Policies*, WHO, Geneva, 1988.

28. Turshen, M. and Thébaud, A., op. cit.

29. Jacoby, E. H., 'The Problem of Transnational Corporations within the UN System' in Steppacher et al. (eds), *Economics in Institutional Perspective*, Lexington Books, 1977.

30. *The Selection of Essential Drugs*, Technical Report Series 615, 641, WHO, Geneva, 1977 and 1979.

31. *International Ethical Guidelines for Biomedical Research Involving Human Subjects*, CIOMS/WHO, Geneva, 1993.

32. Melrose, D., *Bitter Pills*, op. cit.

33. Jayasuriya, D. C., *The Public Health and Economic Dimensions of the New Drug Policy of Bangladesh*, Pharmaceutical Manufacturers Association, Washington DC, September 1985.

34. Various internal memoranda of WHO initiated by A. Wehrli, PHA, and Dr John Dunne between 1991 and 1993.

35. Dunne, John, memorandum to Steiner Holland, DAP, WHO, Geneva, 5 January 1994.

7

Not the end of the story

National health policy

The Expert Committee responsible for the formulation of the National Drug Policy (NDP) in 1982 pointed out at the time: 'If the essential drugs are not readily available at reasonable cost, the national objective of Health for All by the year 2000 cannot be achieved. In the context of our scarce resources and [the] urgency of implementation of a health programme, it is all the more important that a national drug policy be formulated as a part of national health policy.'[1] Contrary to its own wisdom, the Expert Committee had to proceed with formulating the NDP independently of a national health policy.

It was another five years before a four-member presidential committee was appointed – on 18 March 1987 – to formulate a national health policy (NHP). Its four members were Major General M. R. Chowdhury, director of the Army Institute of Pathology and Blood Transfusion Services (Chairman); Professor S. I. M. G. Mannan, a renowned and respected former professor of anatomy, a former president of the Pakistan Medical Association and presently a member of the Executive Committee of the Bangladesh Medical Association (Member Secretary); Professor M. Yunus, an economist and Managing Director of the world-famous Grameen Bank; and Dr Zafrullah Chowdhury of Gonoshasthaya Kendra (GK). The committee submitted its report to the President of the Republic on 25 August 1988.

The salient features of the proposed national health policy were:

- decentralisation of health and family planning activities and administration with the establishment of Health Authorities at regional, district and Upazila levels. Members of these were to be

145

drawn from elected local leaders, doctors and nurses and their professional associations, women's organisations, freedom fighters and journalists. All powers of centralised administration were to be delegated to the proposed Health Authorities;

- integration of health and family planning departments and re-naming of the Ministry of Health and Population Control as the Ministry of Health and Family Welfare;
- an increase in the government's health budget from 2.5 per cent to 10 per cent within five years of enactment of the policy;
- people's participation in the management of Health Authorities through contributing to the services provided. School children, physically disabled persons, the poor and the destitute were to be guaranteed free health care;
- the introduction of a Medical Audit, and the registration of all doctors, nurses, technicians, unqualified village doctors, medical assistants, private hospitals, clinics and diagnostic centres. A referral system was to be introduced to ensure secondary and tertiary care for all citizens, irrespective of their place of residence;
- the introduction of community-based medical education and auto-nomy of all medical institutions to ensure responsibility, authority and accountability of the medical profession;
- measures to ensure equal opportunities for health professionals working in rural and urban areas;
- the abolition of private practice for all teachers in government medical colleges and postgraduate institutes and for trainee doctors up to the level of junior consultant (equivalent to senior registrar in the British National Health Service or chief resident in the US health system) in order to ensure efficiency and proper use of government hospital facilities. To compensate for the loss of private practice, a salary increase of 150% for all medical teachers and the provision of free housing, transport and tele-phone were recommended. Raising of the retirement age from 57 years to 65 years for medical professors and 60 for all others was also recommended. Junior consultants were to be given a 100 per cent salary increase plus other facilities. However, private practice among non-government doctors and retired government doctors was not restricted. Rather, to ensure the delivery of primary health care, junior doctors were encouraged to set up their private practices at the village level, with the incentives of monthly remuneration and a special loan facility to be provided by the government;
- the introduction of laws to ensure quality health care and

compensation to persons who have suffered as a result of negligence by the medical profession;
• the introduction of various legislative and administrative measures:
to ensure the registration of births, deaths and marriages; to
promote breast feeding, ensure that underprivileged and vulner-
able families have adequate food and nutrition, and discourage
early marriage and smoking; and to end the promotion of
addictive drugs and narcotics, the sale of cigarettes to minors and
young people, and the manufacture and sale of substandard or
spurious medicines, medicinal ingredients, excipients, cosmetics,
food and food products, and the sale of harmful pesticides.

At the opening of the winter session of Parliament in January 1990,
President Ershad outlined the NHP and announced the renamed
Ministry of Health and Family Welfare. The opposition parties made
no public comment. They privately admitted that this was a good
policy but doubted whether the government would ever introduce it
in Parliament.

Seven months later, Dr Azizur Rahman, the Minister for Health
and Family Welfare and a former member of the NDP Expert
Committee, introduced the policy in a bill in Parliament and said
that the policy would be formally enacted on 17 October if the bill
was passed. However, events were to ensure that the policy never
became law.

Protests and attacks

The same evening, the Bangladesh Medical Association (BMA) called
for a 72-hour strike by all doctors in protest at what it termed an
anti-people health policy. The executive body cancelled without
notice the general membership of Drs Azizur Rahman, S. I. M. G.
Mannan and Zafrullah Chowdhury, for their role in the formulation
of the policy. The three expelled doctors were given no opportunity
to defend their roles as formulators of the NHP.[2] The strike continued with the support of the opposition political parties.

On 27 October 1990, a group of hooligans attacked and burnt
the office, stores and vehicles of Gonoshasthaya Pharmaceutical Ltd
(GPL). Tension mounted and a month later, on 27 November, Dr
Shamsul Alam Khan Milon, Joint Secretary of the BMA, was killed
by an assassin's bullet while passing through Dhaka University
campus in a rickshaw.

Politicians immediately seized the opportunity offered by the doctors' strike and Dr Milon's death to mobilise protests which continued to escalate and ultimately led to the fall of the Ershad government on 6 December 1990. President Ershad handed over power to the Chief Justice of the Bangladesh Supreme Court, Shahabuddin Ahmed, who then formed an interim government. The president of the BMA, Professor M. A. Majed, was appointed Health Advisor (Minister) in the interim government.

On the very first day of the interim government, Parliament was dissolved and the NHP bill was cancelled by the acting President.

The loss of the health policy was highly regrettable. However, in the political turmoil that ensued, it began to look as if the NDP would also be lost as it, and many of its strongest proponents, came under renewed attack. The BMA called for the cancellation of the NDP (which it also termed an anti-people policy), an investigation into GK and a government takeover of both GK and GPL.[3] It also demanded the arrest of Dr Zafrullah Chowdhury of GK and Dr Azizur Rahman, the erstwhile health minister who had introduced the NHP bill.[4] BASS (the Bangladesh Association of Pharmaceutical Industries) supported the BMA's demand for an investigation into GK and GPL.

The NDP was not withdrawn, but a six-member committee under the chairmanship of Major General Anis Waiz was announced by the health minister on 9 February 1991 to carry out an investigation into GK, GPL, and the Bangladesh Association of Voluntary Sterilisation, a non-governmental organisation (NGO) of which Dr Azizur Rahman was President. Major General Anis Waiz was known for his virulent opposition to the NDP. Dr Majed ordered the cancellation of Dr Zafrullah Chowdhury's membership of the Drug Control Committee and the Drug Pricing Committee.

Political stability began to return to the country following elections in February 1991. Begum Khaleda Zia was sworn in as Prime Minister in March 1991 and Parliament was convened a month later. However, on the last day of April 1991, another emergency struck as a cyclone devastated the southern part of Bangladesh. In the midst of this disaster, the NDP survived one of the most rigorous tests since its introduction.

A consultative meeting with NGOs and foreign diplomats was held, to address the need for the provision of effective relief to the victims of the cyclone. At this meeting, which was presided over by the new prime minister, diplomats from Switzerland and the USA said that their aeroplanes were already loaded with medicine and baby food, and ready to fly into Bangladesh, but that the country's drug policy created on obstacle.

All the ambassadors and other participants were stunned by Khaleda Zia's prompt reply. She said that she greatly appreciated the prompt offer to provide assistance but that any medicine brought into Bangladesh must conform with the essential drugs list. Because of the emergency and the scale of need she instructed the director of the Drug Administration to be available around the clock to advise on the country's drug needs.

The threatening cloud had passed over the NDP; if not permanently, at least for the time being.

The National Drug Policy under attack again

It was a short-lived respite. In the midst of sensitive negotiations with the World Bank over loans for industrial development, the new government faced continued pressure from the BMA for the withdrawal of the 'anti-people drug policy'. The Foreign Investors Chamber of Commerce and Industry (FICCI) also demanded a review of the NDP. The leader of FICCI at the time was S. H. Kabir, Managing Director of Pfizer (Bangladesh) Ltd.

On 6 March 1992, the government announced a 15-member Review Committee, chaired by the secretary of the Ministry of Health and Family Welfare, to review the National Drug Policy of 1982 (NDP 82) and formulate a revised drug policy by 30 April 1992. Among 14 other members, four were medical teachers, three from the pharmaceutical industry, two from the army and one from the Chemists and Druggists Association. The deputy secretary of the ministry, the director of the Drug Administration, the president of the BMA, and two MPs were also made members of the committee. One MP, Dr Mohammed Quamruzzaman, had formerly been a professor of psychiatry, and another, Abdullah Wazed, alias Abdu Mia, was the owner of a small ill-reputed pharmaceutical company, Millat Chemicals, which produced both allopathic and traditional medicines.

At the time the Review Committee was being formed one influential weekly made an astute observation: 'Interestingly, no strong demand has been made by the opposition to change the drug policy of the former regime. Yet the government seems to be attaching much importance to the issue'.[5]

One section of the World Bank, however, did consider the review important. In April 1992, Abid Hasan, Head of the Industry and Energy Unit of the World Bank's office in Bangladesh, met relevant government officials to discuss negotiations for an industrial sector loan. He followed up the meeting with a letter to Ayub Quadri,

Joint Secretary of the government's Economic Relations Division, in which he made five specific recommendations pertaining to pharmaceuticals. World Bank recommendations, especially when loans are being negotiated, are in reality directives to Third World governments. The recommendations were:

- to allow introduction of new products by using free sales certificates;
- to lift all control on prices;
- to remove the control over advertising from the drug licensing authority;
- to remove existing restrictions on foreign firms in the area of choice of products they can produce;
- to abolish controls on the import of pharmaceutical raw materials.

At about the same time, FICCI presented the health minister, Chowdhury Kamal Ibne Yusuf, with a set of proposed amendments to the NDP. These were:

- easier registration of new medicines for local production or importation;
- withdrawal of price control: doctors' choice of drugs to prescribe and market competition were deemed a better means of price control;
- free importation of raw materials without prior approval by the Drug Administration;
- licensing of transnational companies to produce antacids and oral vitamins and an end to discrimination between national and transnational companies.
- protection of TNCs' product patents through the strengthening of intellectual property laws.

In fact, FICCI simply echoed the recommendations of the World Bank, with one small exception. It was not concerned about the removal of controls over advertising as drug companies were already printing and distributing – with impunity – product showcards giving misleading or untrue information. Materials of this kind were often given clearance by the Drug Administration because of its lack of knowledge and training, and because of the regular payment of bribes and 'gifts'.

Confusion over World Bank's position

Concern over these developments led WHO and Unicef to defend the NDP. The country representatives of both organisations wrote to the head of the World Bank in Bangladesh, Christopher Willoughby.[6] The WHO representative wrote: 'Bangladesh initiated the National Drug Policy in 1982, which was very much appreciated, due to its ability to provide low-cost and price-controlled basic essential drugs, affordable by the majority of the population, ensuring a cost-effective process in primary health care'.[7] Both WHO and Unicef recognised the need to update and strengthen the policy, but were calling on the World Bank to ensure that gains that had been secured by the NDP were not undermined.

The strategy worked, up to a point. Abid Hasan, Head of the Industry and Energy Unit of the World Bank's Bangladesh office, was ordered to send another letter to Ayub Quadri, Joint Secretary of the government's Economic Relations Division, clarifying the World Bank's position on the NDP. His letter of 8 June 1992 (Appendix 2) was cleverly written. It began with the statement, 'First and most important, we fully support the drug policy objective of increasing the supply of essential drugs (EDs) and making these available at affordable prices'. It went on to argue that the present controls could be replaced by more liberal policies and procedures 'without sacrificing the objective of increasing availability of good quality and affordable EDs'. The five recommendations were repeated, albeit in a modified form.

The final paragraph was a veiled threat: 'We would appreciate if these views are brought to the attention of the drug policy review committee urgently, specially since one aspect (import controls) of the above is germane to ISAC-II [Industrial Sector Adjustment Credit-II] negotiations.'

Even with the changes, this letter still promoted foreign commercial interests rather than the health interests of the people. At the time, another division of the World Bank's office in Bangladesh – the Population and Health Unit – was finalising agreement with the government and with major donor agencies on a five-year programme that included a significant component on the rational use of drugs and stressed the need to support the National Drug Policy through education and information activities. This effort was subsequently referred to in the World Bank's 1993 report, *Investing in Health*, as a prime example of donor co-operation in planning better health programmes.

The confusion caused by these two World Bank positions was unhelpful. A spokesperson for a major donor agency in Bangladesh said that 'there should have been a public denunciation of the position' of Abid Hasan.[8]

The Review Committee's deliberations drag on

At its first meeting the Review Committee was unable to reach a consensus about the terms of reference for the review of the National Drug Policy of 1982 (NDP 82). Taking advantage of the situation, the chairman formed a subcommittee with five members, three of whom were connected with the drug industry, to prepare a draft of a new National Drug Policy (NDP 92). Dr Majed, the president of the BMA, was made convenor while Brigadier Mukhlesur Rahman Khan, the director of the Drug Administration, became member secretary. It is interesting to note that the subcommittee was asked to draft a new policy, rather than to review NDP 82.

In July 1992, the BMA published an advertisement requesting professionals and ordinary people to submit their suggestions for the formulation of a people-oriented health policy and for changes and expansion of the drug policy in line with current needs.[9]

The term of the Review Committee was extended by another six months to 31 October 1992. Two days before that date, the drug review subcomittee agreed a draft National Drug Policy (NDP 92). It was little more than a comouflaged and elaborate version of the recommendations in Abid Hasan's letter and of those in the memorandum sent by the Foreign Investors Chamber of Commerce and Industry (FICCI).

The subcommittee recommended the creation of a Drug Registration Advisory Committee (DRAC) in place of the Drug Control Committee (DCC), comprising experts from the disciplines of medicine, pharmacology and pharmacy, and representatives from the manufacturers and other trades and professional groups. The expression 'professional groups' would effectively exclude consumer groups but open the gate to a number of groups, directly or indirectly related to the industry, with professional and vested interests. The DRAC would be authorised to approve the addition to the essential drugs list of any drug of proven safety, efficacy and quality. It would determine patterns of disease prevalence and therapeutic need. The subcommittee was particularly concerned to prepare a list of over-the-counter drugs which were to be sold without prescription for the short-term relief of symptoms when medical advice and accurate diagnosis were not required. Obviously, self-prescription and self-purchase fit well with the World Bank's structural adjustment programme. The subcommittee's other main recommendations are given below and the number in parenthesis is the section number of the report:

- promotion of under-licence manufacturing (4.4) and special incentives to foreign companies to set up manufacturing plants to encourage production of their 'research-based' new products (4.5);
- protection of intellectual property rights (4.10);
- removal of the requirement of prior approval for the importation of raw and packaging materials (10.1);
- the setting of their own MRP by manufacturers (10.3);
- separate administration of traditional medicines 'which should not be amalgamated with allopathic drugs at any level be it manufacturers or dispensaries' (12).

NDP 92 was not able to make its maiden voyage. In November 1992, the traditional medical systems together sued the Ministry of Health and Family Welfare and the director of the Drug Administration, claiming that the Review Committee was invalid as it included no traditional practitioners. The court issued a stay order, preventing the government from giving any further consideration to the report.

A lull in the storm?

For almost a year, it appeared that the main elements of the NDP would survive, even if attempts were still being made to erode some of its provisions. One of the major proponents of change, the BMA, went quiet about the NDP. It did not make any comment on either NDP 82 or the proposed NDP 92 in its own draft of a national health policy, released to BMA members in 1993.[10] In late 1993, the BMA submitted a charter of 21 demands to the prime minister which did not include their usual clarion call for cancellation of the 'anti-people drug policy'.

In mid-October 1993, the BMA president, Dr M. A. Majed, and general secretary, Dr Gazi Abdul Haque, even issued a press release which denounced attempts to deregulate drug pricing. They claimed that current drug prices were within the reach of common people and that while prices of other commodities had gone up, drug prices had not increased proportionately. They agreed with the need for a review of the NDP, but not with the withdrawal of price controls.[11]

A bigger threat to the NDP in 1993 came from Bangladesh's finance minister, M. Saifur Rahman. He believed that the NDP was a major impediment to foreign investment in Bangladesh. He told a seminar on the 'Present status and future prospects of the Bangladesh Pharmaceutical Industry' run by BASS on 12 October

1993 that NDP 82 should be 'immediately scrapped' and that the policy was 'ruining the blue-chip pharmaceutical industry'.[12] He added that the industry should be free of all controls.

About a week later, the health minister said in a meeting that the government might review the drug policy. That was sufficient warning for representatives from WHO and Unicef to approach Christopher R. Willoughby, Head of the World Bank Resident Mission in the country. The three heads of mission wrote a joint letter to Shameen Ahsan, Secretary of Health and Family Welfare, (Appendix 3), which they copied to the finance minister, Saifur Rahman, and the health minister, Chowdhury Kamal Ibne Yusuf. In this they said that the World Bank and other relevant UN agencies considered Bangladesh's National Drug Policy of 1982 to be a good policy which had had a major positive impact on the health situation of the country as well as favourable consequences for the economics of the pharmaceutical industry.

They also had a meeting with the finance minister and the health minister the following week. Saifur Rahman was visibly angry and asked why the three men had come together. To threaten him? To frighten him? And which directive should he comply with: Abid Hasan's or theirs? Willoughby replied that Abid Hasan's letter of 8 June 1992 had been sent without proper clearance and proceeded to reiterate the World Bank's and other UN agencies' support for the NDP.

After this meeting, Saifur Rahman realised that it was not possible to kill NDP 82 in one go and that a change of strategy was necessary. Instead of attempting formally to abandon the basic principle of a limited list of essential drugs, it was decided to unban a number of drugs at every meeting of the Drug Control Committee, chaired by Shameen Ahsan.

Eroding the National Drug Policy

Since the Drug Control Committee (DCC) had been reconstituted in early 1992, a pattern of new approvals for drugs was set in motion. An abundance of new members representing the drug industry helped ensure decisions favourable to the industry. At the first meeting, in March 1992, a non-essential combination cough rub, Vaporub, was approved, along with 12 other single-ingredient products of no proven superiority over existing ones. Three of the drugs were not even recorded in the British Pharmacopoeia, the US Pharmacopoeia or *Martindale: The Extra Pharmacopoeia*.

In June 1992, Pfizer won an appeal decision to get two drugs that had been banned under NDP 82 back on the market: Unasyn (ampicillin plus salbactum) and Daricon (oxyphencyclamine).

In late 1992, a DCC meeting that was barely quorate, and attended mainly by members from the pharmaceutical industry, took two important decisions that violated the principles of the drug policy. During discussions under the agenda item 'Miscellaneous', it was decided to allow products such as antacids and simethicone, multivitamins with minerals, and vitamin B-complex syrup. The argument put forward was that since Ayurvedic and Unani manufacturers were cheating rural people with their primitive tonics concocted from herbs and minerals, it was better to allow allopathic drug producers to manufacture these products.

One young pharmacologist representing the BMA tried to resist, but he was too junior to be taken seriously by the health secretary and the president of BASS. When he informed the BMA of what was happening, Dr Majed told him that the issue would be settled with the introduction of NDP 92, which would soon be submitted to the government. Over the next three months, a number of vitamin B-complex syrups appeared on the market, including B12 in 100ml bottles, at Taka 43 per bottle. The number of new products registered for manufacture grew at a faster rate than before: more than 150 products in an eight-month period (Table 7.1).

Since the end of 1992, consumers have started protesting about the release on to the market of many of the ineffective and highly priced drugs banned by NDP 82, especially vitamin B-complex syrup.[13]

In October 1993, a high-powered committee under the chairman-

Table 7.1: Number of manufacturing units in 1992 and increase in registered medicinal products in the period December 1991–August 1992

Type of system	Number of manufacturing units	Registered medicinal products	
		December 1991	August 1992
Allopathic	199	4,471	4,625*
Unani	237	670	1,320
Ayurvedic	171	3,150	3,506
Homeopathic	61	650	750

* With 871 importable registered products total, the number of registered products is 5,496 inclusive of all formulations and dosage forms.

Source: Bangladesh Administration, 1992

ship of the deputy leader of Parliament, Dr A. Q. M. Badruddoza Chowdhury, was set up to review the list of drugs banned under NDP 82. The committee was given a month to submit its report but was unable to reach a conclusion.[14]

Limited price control

The price of drugs is a sensitive issue and the question of de-regulation of prices could not easily be raised without an adverse reaction from both consumers and professionals. To get round this problem, it was proposed that a small list of essential drugs should remain regulated and that other drugs should not be subject to any kind of price control. A committee chaired by Professor Nurun Nabi, Director General of Health Services, was formed to finalise this smaller list of essential drugs.[15] The six-member committee was composed of three doctors, two pharmacists and the president of BASS (who also owns Beximco), the majority of whom were well known for their opposition to NDP 82.

The Nurun Nabi Committee met on 11 January 1994, and submitted its recommendations on the same day. These were:

1. A list of 117 drugs (referred to as 'listed drugs') should be subjected to price control. Twenty-six of these were contraceptives, intravenous solutions and vaccines.

    (The term 'listed drugs' was introduced to describe this new list in order to avoid the definitional problems associated with the concept of essential drugs as well as to bypass the High Court's restrictions imposed on amendments to the essential drugs list. The list was an arbitrary one and the criteria for inclusion on it were not defined by the committee. High-selling common drugs such as cimetidine, ranitidine, diclofenac, cephalosporins, antihistamines (excluding chlorpheniramine), irrational combinations of vitamins and minerals, and antacids and simethicone, as well as expensive newer drugs, were not included.)

2. No imports of drugs produced locally should be allowed.

3. Price control of imported raw and packaging materials should be discontinued. Manufacturers of drugs not included in the list should be free to fix their own price (referred to as the 'indicative price') and inform the Drug Administration of this.

4. Every manufacturer should ensure that 60 per cent of the drugs it produces are listed drugs. (How this was to be ensured was not explained by the committee.)

Honourable Prime Minister, 'Medicine is not a Shampoo'

Madam Prime Minister, we know that, you do not consider medicine as a Shampoo, but your Finance Minister (FM) Saifur Rahman does. He puts Shampoo, Chocolat, Coca-Cola and Medicines in the same basket of commodity.

The FM is trying to dismantle the *National Drug Policy (NDP)* and the existing price fixation procedures for drugs, claiming that NDP is the main deterrent for foreign investment in Bangladesh. This is misleading and false. **We challenge Saifur Rahman to disclose the names of foreign or local investors who decline investment in Bangladesh on account of NDP!**

The Chiefs of the World Bank, UNICEF and World Health Organization in Bangladesh have called on FM in November, 1993 to uphold the principles of the NDP. They wrote-

> **'... there seems to be unanimity among international health expert that this policy has had a major positive impact on the health situation of this country with favourable consequences for the economics of the pharmaceutical industry. The Essential Drugs Policy has also given Bangladesh the image, in other countries, of being a progressive nation providing enlightened leadership in this vital area of Health of All.**

The causes of the lack of foreign investment are his jungle economics, high banded bureaucracy, political anarchy, and above all, lack of democratic practice and tolerance.

Drugs Pricing System was devised in 1978 by 4-members committee under the chairmanship of Prof. M.A. Mannan (former Vice-Chancellor of Dhaka University and Chairman, Pharmacy Dept.). The President of the Bangladesh Ausudh Silpa Samity, Salman Rahman, was also a member of that committee.

Madam Prime Minister, People have rejected Saifur Rahman in the last democratic election of 1991, but the election showed that *you have the love and respect of people.* Is it possible that people like Saifur Rahman are systematically executing and propagating anti-people activities to destroy your image? Or is he just taking revenge on the people as they did not vote for him?

In the last budget, FM imposed 'No Import Tax' for helicopters, while 30% import duties plus 15% VAT imposed on microbuses and trucks. **But 45% import duty plus VAT and other taxes amounting to a total of almost 72% are charged on ambulances. Irrational duties are also charged on medical and research equipments.** Whose interest is Saifur Rahman serving? Clearly, he is not serving the national interest.

Medicines which are harmful, dangerous and useless for health have started entering the market again. The decision on such an important issue as essential drugs and drug policy should be made by Parliament not by administrative order. Saifur Rahman is bypassing the Parliament. It will be quite devastating for your popularity and your government to endorse administrative orders formulated behind closed door by Saifur Rahman and a few of the friends.

Honourable Prime Minister, medicine is not a shampoo. It does not wash away like a shampoo. Whatever decisions you take about health and essential drugs will have a lasting effect on people. People will remember this all the time especially at the time of next election.

Health is a crucial political entry point to reach closer to the people.

Health For All
4 Green Square, Green Road
Dhaka-1205. Tel: 500383

5. To ensure sufficient production of 'listed products', duties on unlisted drugs may be raised to 15 per cent (from 7.5 per cent).
6. As price control of imported and locally produced raw materials and packing materials would be abolished, tariff protection of 30 per cent should be given to local manufacturers of raw and packaging materials to safeguard their interests.

The Nurun Nabi Committee's recommendations were presented to the Drug Control Committee on 12 January 1994 without prior inclusion in the agenda.[16] The member representing the BMA, a junior pharmacologist, raised questions about the criteria for the new 'listed drugs' and their relationship to essential drugs, and about the differential pricing of drugs belonging to the same therapeutic group. Shameen Ahsan's response was that the proposal had been prepared by a highly qualified committee and that it referred to listed drugs not an essential drugs list. The Director-General of Health Services remained silent as he had already been urged to comply, on assurance of other benefits including the extension of his job beyond the retirement age of 57.[17] Shameen Ahsan succeeded in getting the DCC to agree to the first four recommendations. The last two were rejected because they ran counter to the policy of liberalisation and the ideology of the free market economy.

An extensive press campaign by the local organisation Health For All (HFA) succeeded in delaying the execution of the recommendations until June 1994. One advertisement placed by HFA – entitled 'Honourable Prime Minister, "Medicine is not a Shampoo",' and taking the form of an open letter to the Prime Minister (Appendix 4) – attracted so much attention that many newspapers and periodicals published the advertisement free of charge. A Bengali version appeared in Bengali newspapers and periodicals.

As expected, the prices of drugs which are not 'listed' have started shooting up. HFA, the Consumer Association of Bangladesh and various newspapers have raised questions as to why there are two prices for the same drug. Of particular concern are Ciba-Geigy's Volteran (diclofenac) and Glaxo's Zantac (ranitidine), whose prices are four to six times higher than other brands of the same drugs.

'A noble experiment'

The Bangladesh National Drug Policy has been both praised and attacked over the years. It has survived a series of onslaughts from vested interests that should have destroyed it completely. Yet there are still parts of the policy in place.

Consumer organisations, health activists and a few journalists are struggling together to retain the benefits which the country achieved through the drug policy. On behalf of HFA, lawyers prepared a public interest case against the Bangladesh government for violation of various provisions of NDP 82. The case was filed at the High Court in early 1995.

In 1992, Milton Silverman and his colleagues described the efforts of the people of Bangladesh to craft a successful National Drug Policy as a 'noble experiment', one which had been 'widely acclaimed', 'applauded' and 'enthusiastically depicted as the forerunner of similar programs destined to sweep throughout the Third World'.[18] They also noted that the experiment had yet to be adopted in full by another country and concluded enigmatically: 'The end of the chapter is yet to be written.'[19]

So too with the National Drug Policy itself. Much has been achieved; much remains to be done. Clearly there is a need for a tighter policy.

Virtually every year since the NDP was adopted there has been prominent coverage – front-page reports and inside-page editorials in both daily newspapers and periodicals – of substandard, counterfeit and spurious drugs, the sale of expired drugs, the smuggling of banned drugs, the preponderance of unauthorised retail pharmacies, the increased price of drugs above the maximum retail price (MRP) and the inadequacy of legal provision to control all these violations. The need for a review of NDP 82, and the conspiracy against the policy, have been extensively discussed.

Not one popular newspaper has called for the withdrawal or suspension of NDP 82. Significantly, there has also been no call for the NDP to be fully implemented. Much of the debate around the policy has focused on banned drugs and the essential drugs list. However, NDP 82 contained a series of recommendations that, had they been put into effect, might have led to a different drug situation in Bangladesh today, and to a different debate.

The problem of quality assurance

A perennial problem has been the assurance of quality of drugs. In 1982 there were some 14,000 retail pharmacies in Bangladesh. By 1993 there were more than 60,000. During the same time period the number of supervisory officers went up from 32 to only 38.

Their job is to monitor drug promotion, visit drug firms, collect samples from retail shops and conduct bi-annual inspections of manufacturing premises in order to decide whether or not to renew manufacturing licences. It was impossible for them to do the job in 1982, let alone now.

Graduate pharmacists are in short supply. Because of budgetary constraints, it was recommended in NDP 82 that all existing Upazila (Thana) Health Administrators be empowered to inspect and monitor all retail pharmacies, wholesalers and drug pedlars in their operational areas and take action if necessary. Unfortunately this recommendation was not put into practice.

NDP 82 also recommended the establishment of another central national drug control laboratory for the quality testing of traditional medicines and for development of specifications on these. This has yet to be implemented.

At present, decisions made by the government drug-testing laboratory cannot be challenged, a situation which is of course unfair. There should be an appeal system in place so that the Drug Licensing Authority could appoint an independent scientific observer to oversee a repeat analysis if a manufacturer disagrees with the findings of the laboratory. The costs of this could be borne by the manufacturer initially; if the new analysis results in a favourable finding for the manufacturer, these costs should be reimbursed.

Quality assurance begins at the production stage, however. Within Bangladesh there have been no initiatives to help small manufacturers establish a properly equipped and staffed quality control laboratory on a collective basis in each area. Laboratories are attached to individual small companies, although often they exist in name only as the majority are non-operative.

NDP 82 recommended heavier penalties, including confiscation of equipment, for companies persistently manufacturing substandard drugs. The definition of substandard in Bangladesh is not rational. Even if it has an adequate quantity of ingredients a medicinal product is defined as substandard if it is wrongly labelled or packaged. Although such an item should definitely be withdrawn from the market the product itself should not be termed substandard. This term should specifically be applied to a product which fails to match up to the declared content, with a maximum variation of 5 per cent. In the case of substandard drugs, there is an elaborate process of public notification, and the offending drugs are collected and taken to the Drug Administration for destruction. The product must be de-registered for at least three years if it contains less than 80 per cent of the declared content.

In the public interest, any company which consistently produces substandard drugs – for example, producing within one year two or more products with less than 80 per cent of the declared amount of ingredients – should have its manufacturing licence revoked for at least three years.

Quality assurance procedures for imported drugs and raw materials are also deficient at present. In an ideal world, WHO would be able to organise a thorough independent inspection of factories producing raw materials and finished drugs and be able to assure the quality of products from such factories. As it is, a recent evaluation of WHO's own Certification Scheme on the Quality of Pharmaceutical Products Moving in International Commerce found that it is not being applied to most products.[20] Demanding such a certificate for all imports is one way to improve quality; so too is the regular testing of samples of imported drugs and raw materials.

If measures such as these had been put into place over the years since the adoption of NDP 82, many of the concerns about drug quality in Bangladesh might now be history. However, this has not happened, and we continue to face an uncertain future about the quality of drugs.

The need for tighter registration controls

That uncertainty also extends to the selection of drugs on the market. An increasing flood of products is coming on to the market, many of which were banned in 1982. The most crucial omission of the Drug (Control) Ordinance 1982 is that although the schedule of banned drugs was annexed with the ordinance, the NDP policy document itself was not formally incorporated. Lists of essential drugs and supplementary drugs were not made an integral part of the Ordinance. These are observed or adhered to under administrative orders, not by legislative requirements.

Similarly, the composition of the Drug Control Committee (DCC) and criteria for registration of a drug were not detailed in the Ordinance. Thus, the decisions being made today about which drugs to allow on the market, and the people who should be allowed to make those decisions, are more difficult to challenge.

Certainly, these are not decisions that should be made by people with a vested interest in the pharmaceutical industry. In most countries with a strong regulatory authority, a committee such as the DCC would be made up of independent medical professionals, clinical pharmacologists, and pharmacists. Representatives from consumer and women's organisations may also be included as observers.

All countries exercise judgement over which drugs to allow on their markets. Medical need and cost-effectiveness are important criteria for evaluating a drug for registration but were not mentioned in the Drug (Control) Ordinance 1982. For there to be clear, transparent procedures for the registration of drugs in Bangladesh, the DCC should use two basic guidelines for allowing a new drug:

- if its claims to increased safety, efficacy and cost-effectiveness are supported by clinical trials acceptable to the DCC. An improved dosing schedule and reduced potential for abuse or inappropriate use should be considered additional benefits;
- if there is no drug on the market with similar therapeutic action or if the new drug has a better risk:benefit ratio and is cheaper than an existing equivalent.

Unfinished business

Measures to deal with these two areas of quality assurance and transparency of registration decisions would do much to clear up the controversy that still lingers over NDP 82. The mere existence of that controversy demonstrates how much more there is to do to ensure that people in Bangladesh have access to the essential drugs they need to treat their illnesses. Meanwhile, the groups which have opposed the drug policy since its introduction continue their efforts to undermine it. TNCs and local producers alike, backed by the World Bank, are pressing for deregulation and liberalisation.

Milton Silverman and his colleagues said 'the end of the chapter is yet to be written'. In the early 1990s, that end often looked as if it might be a summary execution. Subsequently, the end seemed to be being written as a gradual erosion of the basic principles upon which NDP 82 was based.

But there is another possible ending, an ending that puts people's health first, that delivers essential drugs, that encourages a strong pharmaceutical sector to operate within reasonable regulations to ensure that public health concerns are foremost. This is the ending envisaged in 1982 when the National Drug Policy was drafted. The struggle to achieve this goal continues.

Notes

1. Expert Committee, *Evaluation of Registered/Licensed Products and Draft National Drug Policy*, Dhaka, 11 May 1982.
2. 'Membership cancelled', *Daily Sangbad*, Dhaka, 28 July 1990.
3. 'BMA demands trial of Aziz, Zafrullah', *Daily Sangbad*, Dhaka, 18 December 1990, and *Bangladesh Observer*, Dhaka, 20 December 1990.
4. 'BMA demands arrest of Dr Zafrullah Chowdhury and Dr Azizur Rahman and cancellation of all committees of Health Ministry', *Ittefaq* and other Dhaka newspapers, 20 December 1990.
5. 'Drug Policy once more: Does the Drug Policy need a healing touch?', *Weekly Dhaka Courier*, Dhaka, 1-7 May 1992.
6. 'A back-to-square-one Drug Policy: WB proposes, UNICEF, WHO oppose', *Weekly Dhaka Courier*, 4 December 1992.
7. 'A back to square one Drug Policy: WB proposes, UNICEF, WHO oppose', op. cit.
8. Chetley, A., 'From Policy to Practice', IOCU, Penang, 1992, p. 45.
9. Advertisement by Bangladesh Medical Association, *Ittefaq*, Dhaka, 12 July 1992.
10. 'Draft National Health Policy (for members consideration)', Bangladesh Medical Association, Dhaka, 31 May 1993.
11. Majed, M. A. and Haque, G. A., press release BMA/15, Bangladesh Medical Association, Dhaka, 15 October 1993.
12. 'Scrap '82 drug policy', *Morning Sun*, 13 October 1993.
13. 'Manufacture of illegal Vit B-Complex: Drug body trying to scuttle Law', *New Nation*, 12 September 1993.
14. Ministry of Health and Family Welfare, 'Notification Public Health-1/Drugs-18/94/43/(19)', Government of People's Republic of Bangladesh, Dhaka, 8 February 1994.
15. Government of Bangladesh, Health and Family Welfare Ministry, Office notification: public health/drugs, 9/93, 30 December 1993.
16. Proceedings of 195th meeting of the Drug Control Committee held on 12 January 1994.
17. Nurun, Nabi, Director, General Health Services, Bangladesh, discussion with author at WHA, Geneva, 6 May 1994.
18. Silverman, M., Lydecker, M. and Lee, P.R., *Bad Medicine: The Prescription Drug Industry in the Third World*, Stanford University Press, California, 1992.
19. Ibid.
20. WHO, *Use of the WHO Certification Scheme on the Quality of Pharmaceutical Products Moving in International Commerce*, WHO/DAP Research Series No. 16, Geneva, 1995.

Appendices

Appendix 1

Letter from Lewis A. Engman, President of the Pharmaceutical Manufacturers Association, to Lt. General Hossain Mohammad Ershad, President of the People's Republic of Bangladesh, dated 16 June 1982.

Dear Mr. Chairman:

The Pharmaceutical Manufacturers Association represents 143 U.S. pharmaceutical manufacturers, several of which have investments in Bangladesh.

We have been informed that the Government of Bangladesh has announced a New Drug Policy as implemented by Drug Control Ordinance 1982 (published on June 12, 1982).

Although we have not yet been able to fully review the complete Ordinance, we understand that it contains a number of provisions which we respectfully suggest could have a negative impact on health care in Bangladesh.

Several of the provisions, such as the use of generic names only, excessively rigid interpretation of the concept of an essential drugs list and undue discrimination against multinational companies, have already been tried and rejected in countries such as Sri Lanka and Pakistan.

Dr. Sanjaya Lall, a Consultant to UNCTAD and other UN agencies and a prominent critic of the large pharmaceutical companies, recently spoke on the pharmaceutical industry in India. He concluded that government policies (several of which are similar to those in the Drug Control Ordinance 1982) have resulted in the added expenditure of scarce foreign exchange and have had a negative impact on foreign investment, the development of the Indian pharmaceutical industry and the availability of quality pharmaceuticals. It would be particularly unfortunate if Bangladesh, which has made such impressive progress in recent years, were to follow the mistaken pharmaceutical policies of such countries.

In addition, a policy of discriminating against foreign investment in the pharmaceutical industry could have a negative impact on Bangdadesh's program to attract foreign investment in general, as well as obviously discouraging such investment in the pharmaceutical industry.

Specifically in terms of the pharmaceutical industry, we have been told by the Bangladesh Association of Pharmaceutical Industries that the following consequences are likely if the Ordinance is enforced:

- Rapid abandonment by leading pharmaceutical companies of currently planned new investment and expansion projects totaling between 15 and 20 million U.S. dollars.
- Shutdown of a number of local pharmaceutical plants, and perhaps some foreign ones.
- A 60 percent curtailment of production by those companies that will be able to remain in business.
- Dismissal of up to 35 percent of their employees for whom few job opportunities will exist. (Counting their families, an estimated 10,000 persons are likely thus to be affected).

PROPOSAL

We therefore respectfully suggest, Mr. Chairman, the following:

1. The implementation of the Drug Control Ordinance 1982, published only a few days ago, be delayed.
2. As the issues at hand are vital both to the well-being of the people of Bangladesh and to the investment climate in your country, a review panel be formed to include delegates selected by and from:

>   The Bangladesh Medical Association
>   The Bangladesh Pharmaceutical Society
>   The Bangladesh Association of Pharmaceutical Industries

We feel, Mr. Chairman, that ample time should be allowed the panel to study the matter in depth and without any outside pressures of any kind.

3. The review panel should also have the freedom of examining and drawing upon the recommendations of the Drug Technical Advisory Board which had been awaiting a review by the Cabinet.

We sincerely believe, Mr. Chairman, that such positive steps will be in the best interests of the public health of Bangladesh and will reinforce the confidence of foreign investors in the New Industrial Policy of your esteemed government.

Respectfully yours,

Appendix 2

Letter from Abid Hasan, Head of the Industry and Energy Unit of the World Bank's Resident Mission in Bangladesh, to Ayub Quadri, Joint Secretary, Economic Relations Division, Government of Bangladesh, dated 8 June 1992 and marked 'Urgent'.

Dear Mr. Quadri:

ISAC-2 : Deregulation related to Drug Industry

In our letter of April 13, we had made several recommendations (Recommendation No. 27-31) related to streamlining import and other economic regulatory controls related to the drug industry. In light of comments made by concerned

GOB officials and development partners on our recommendations, I would like to clarify a few points in regards to our views.

First, and most important, we fully support the drug policy objective of increasing supply of essential drug (EDs) and making these available at affordable prices. However, our view is that the present set of controls/means established to achieve the above objective are cumbersome and discretionary, lead to rent seeking and are redundant in some cases. They could be replaced by policies/ procedures which are non-discretionary and automatic without sacrificing the objective of increasing availability of good quality and affordable EDs.

Let me now discuss our specific recommendation.

Recommendation 27   Allow introduction of new products by using free sales certification.

This recommendation should not be interpreted to mean that we are recommending withdrawal of registration requirements or the evaluation/testing that is required for registration. We understand that registration policy/process gives preferential treatment to EDs and at the same time allows other useful drugs (e.g. rare disease drugs) to be introduced. We fully support this and believe that the registration process should be transparent and not subject to arbitrary decision like that related to establishing an exclusive list of 302 drugs.

Recommendation 28   Lift all controls on prices

Although fixation of flat rate MRP may have contributed to keeping a check on drug prices, the drug industry feels that price controls are redundant as the prices of most drugs are determined by competitive market forces rather than MRP. Flat rate price controls hurts those firms which spend money on quality assurance and maintain good manufacturing practices. While the MRP policy can be enforced at the manufacturing stage, with 35 drug inspectors it is impossible to enforce price control at the retail stage where there are nearly 18,000 pharmacies. It is the generally held view, which we share, that a decontrol of prices would not lead to an abnormal rise in prices because of the competitive structure of the market. We feel serious consideration should be given to lifting price controls, while at the same time strengthening DA's capabilities to monitor price trends at the consumer level. Manufacturers would still be required by law to print their own MRPs on the labels to protect consumer interest. It after price decontrol a firm increases its drug prices, particularly of EDs. abnormally (i.e. price increase is higher than increase in the firm's cost of production and marketing), the existing drug legislation provides adequate legal authority to the Government to intervene.

Recommendation 29   Remove the control over advertising from the drug licensing authority

In this recommendation we are in no way recommending lifting of advertisement controls that are needed to ensure that no false claim are made, toxic side effects suppressed, etc. Such controls should remain. Our recommendation relates to controls on amount of money (5% of sales) that a firm could spend on samples advertising. Such controls infringe on autonomy of firms and their marketing strategy and their removal should be considered. Vigilance regarding ethical standards and disallowing personal gifts and incentives to doctors will continue to be required.

Recommendation 30 <u>Remove existing restrictions on foreign firms in the area of choice of products they can produce.</u>

We continue to believe that disallowing foreign firms to manufacture products made by local firms not only restricts competition but also hurts the governments' policy of encouraging foreign investment. This control should be removed. Foreign firms should operate under the same controls/regulations as the local firms.

Recommendation 31 <u>Abolish the Block List system of approval for import of pharmaceutical raw materials and allow pharmaceutical companies to import their inputs freely.</u>

As we understand, the current control on imports of raw materials is in place to meet the following objectives: increase supply of ED, ensure competitively priced imports with a view to minimize transfer pricing and keep in check prices of final drugs, and ensure imports from authentic manufacturers. We believe the current controls, which are cumbersome and discretionary, could be replaced by a better set of policies/procedures which achieve the above objectives and are at the same time transparent, non-discretionary and automatic. We suggest, for the committee's consideration, the following set of policy changes to replace the existing controls:

(i)   An efficient and non-distortionary tax policy which favours production of EDs, particularly HPC/EDs. A preferred policy is to use direct tax instrument for this purpose. Pending introduction of a direct tax based system, we suggest continuation of the current import taxation policy on active ingredients which favours production of EDs, over non-EDs. Consideration could also be given to further enhancing the favourable tax treatment for active ingredients of PHC/EDs and expanding it to cover active ingredients of secondary/tertiary EDs.

(ii) Based on prevailing international prices of raw materials, collected possibly with help of WHO, the DA could publish maximum allowable import prices for active ingredients which would be made available for checking at the time of clearance. As long as drug firms import value is below this price, they would not be required to get DA's prior approval for imports, as is currently done for each and every consignment.

(iii) All quantitative restrictions (QRs) on inputs to EDs should be lifted, so that no prior permission of DA is needed. QRs on ED inputs runs counter to the policy of encouraging production of such drugs.

(iv) Annually, DA could publish a list of authentic manufacturers from whom active ingredient raw materials could be imported without prior permission. Thus, as long as imports were from firms on this list (prepared in consultation with the industry) no prior approval of DA would be required for most of the raw material imports. Easy procedures would be established to enable new sources could be added to this list during the year. The custom authorities would be required to ensure that no imports of active ingredient imports are allowed from firms that are not on the list.

(v) A maximum value limit on imported inputs for non-ED production. Thus, for example, value of imported inputs for non-ED drugs could be limited to, say 25%, of the total value of a firms' raw material imports. This would ensure that a major share of production is utilized for manufacture of EDs. Compliance to such a rule could be checked once a year by the DA's inspectors rather than on a prior approval basis.

We would appreciate if these views are brought to the attention of the drug policy review committee urgently, specially since one aspect (import controls) of the above is germane to the ISAC-II negotiations.

With kind regards,

Yours sincerely,

Appendix 3

Letter from Rolf C Carriere, UNICEF Representative, Bangladesh; Christopher R. Willoughby, Chief of World Bank's Resident Mission in Bangladesh; A. N. A. Abevesundere, WHO Representative; to Shamin Ahsan, Secretary of the Ministry of Health and Family Welfare, Government of Bangladesh, dated 28 October 1993.

Dear Mr Secretary,

Recent press reports seem to indicate that the Government of Bangladesh is contemplating amendments to the country's Essential Drugs Policy. According to newspaper reports, this appears to be based on the government's alleged dissatisfaction with certain aspects of the functioning of that policy, and the need to open up the country for a free trade and investment in pharmaceuticals.

As the newspaper reports do not always accurately reflect what is said during meetings. We are not sure whether this is indeed the position of the Government.

We would however like to use this opportunity to share with you a recent report, 'From Policy to Practice – The Future of the Bangladesh National Drug Policy' by Andrew Chetley, published from Malaysia in 1992 by the International Organization of Consumers Union. We attach a copy of this, together with a summary in brochure form.

We know how extremely busy you are. Yet, may we request that you spend some five minutes reading the brochure. While no one would deny the need for periodic revisions of such a policy, there seems to be unanimity among international health experts that this policy has had a major positive impact on the health situation of this country with favourable consequences for the economics of the pharmaceutical industry. The Essential Drugs Policy has also given Bangladesh the image, in other countries, of being a progressive nation providing enlightened leadership in this vital area of Health for All.

May we add that UNICEF and the World Bank fully support WHO's Policy on essential drugs; and support its being the basis for revision of the National Drug Policy.

We hope you will find these attachments useful. We will be glad to make ourselves available to discuss the issues with you and other authorities of the government if so desired.

Please accept, the assurances of our highest considerations.

Index